Guided by Principle, Driven by Change

THE ACE SERIES ON HIGHER EDUCATION

Series Editor

Ally Hammond, Senior Director of Marketing and Communications

The American Council on Education (ACE) is a membership organization that leads higher education with a united vision for the future. Since its early history, ACE has contributed to the higher education canon. In collaboration with Bloomsbury Publishing, ACE's book series is specifically tailored to the interests of its members. The ACE Series on Higher Education features books that address and spark dialogue on significant issues that affect college and university campuses.

Selected Titles in Series

Guided by Principle, Driven by Change: Insights on Transformative Leadership from University Presidents Globally edited by Devorah Lieberman

Transforming Higher Education: How Bold and Innovative Leaders Entrepreneur the Future by Mary Landon Darden and Joanna L. Kyle

Using Data Analytics to Drive Transformational Change: The Chapman University Story by James L. Doti

College Student Retention: Formula for Student Success, Third Edition by Alan Seidman

Entrepreneuring the Future of Higher Education: Radical Transformation in Times of Profound Change by Mary Landon Darden

The Indispensable University: Higher Education, Economic Development, and the Knowledge Economy by Eugene P. Trani and Robert D. Holsworth

Assessment for Excellence: The Philosophy and Practice of Assessment and Evaluation in Higher Education, Second Edition by Alexander W. Astin and Anthony Lising Antonio

Performance: The Dynamic of Results in Postsecondary Organizations by Richard L. Alfred, Nathan Harris, Kathryn Thirolf, and James Webb

Faculty Success through Mentoring: A Guide for Mentors, Mentees, and Leaders by Carole J. Bland, Anne L. Taylor, S. Lynn Shollen, Anne Marie Weber-Main, and Patricia A. Mulcahy

Innovations in Higher Education: Igniting the Spark for Success by Allan M. Hoffman and Stephen D. Spangehl

Leading from the Middle: A Case-Study Approach to Academic Leadership for Associate and Assistant Deans by Tammy Stone and Mary Coussons-Read

Learning to Lead: A Handbook for Postsecondary Administrators by James R. Davis

Higher Education Assessments: Leadership Matters by Gary L. Kramer and Randy L. Swing

Academic Turnarounds: Restoring Vitality to Challenged American Colleges/Universities by Terrence MacTaggart

Leadership Legacy Moments: Visions and Values for Stewards of Collegiate Mission by E. Grady Bogue

Managing Diversity Flashpoints in Higher Education by Joseph E. Garcia and Karen J. Hoelscher

Strategic Leadership: Integrating Strategy and Leadership in Colleges and Universities by Richard L. Morrill

The Art and Politics of Academic Governance: Relations among Boards, Presidents, and Faculty by Kenneth P. Mortimer and Colleen O'Brien Sathre

Searching for Higher Education Leadership: Advice for Candidates and Search Committees by Jean A. Dowdall

Other Duties as Assigned: Presidential Assistants in Higher Education by Mark P. Curchack

Leaders in the Crossroads: Success and Failure in the College Presidency by Stephen James Nelson

Out in Front: The College President as the Face of the Institution by Lawrence V. Weill

Beyond 2020: Envisioning the Future of Universities in America by Mary Landon Darden

Guided by Principle, Driven by Change

Insights on Transformative Leadership from University Presidents Globally

Edited by Devorah Lieberman

American Council on Education

BLOOMSBURY ACADEMIC
NEW YORK • LONDON • OXFORD • NEW DELHI • SYDNEY

BLOOMSBURY ACADEMIC
Bloomsbury Publishing Inc, 1359 Broadway, New York, NY 10018, USA
Bloomsbury Publishing Plc, 50 Bedford Square, London, WC1B 3DP, UK
Bloomsbury Publishing Ireland, 29 Earlsfort Terrace, Dublin 2, D02 AY28, Ireland

BLOOMSBURY, BLOOMSBURY ACADEMIC and the Diana logo are trademarks of Bloomsbury Publishing Plc

First published in the United States of America 2026

Cover design by Kathi Ha
Cover images © iStock.com/mikimad and melitas

Library of Congress Cataloging-in-Publication Data is available

ISBN: HB: 979-8-216-38302-4
PB: 979-8-216-38303-1
ePDF: 979-8-216-38301-7
eBook: 979-8-216-38304-8

Series: The ACE Series on Higher Education

Typeset by Integra Software Services Pvt. Ltd.

For product safety related questions contact productsafety@bloomsbury.com.

Contents

Foreword

On behalf of the International Association of University Presidents (IAUP), I am pleased to share with you this work that began in 2023 through the IAUP Women's Leadership Initiative, produced last year as an IAUP book spotlighting global women's leadership, and continues with this new publication that features transformative presidential leaders throughout the world.

Under the leadership of Dr. Devorah Lieberman, president emerita of the University of La Verne, this book focuses on a select group of presidents, rectors, and chancellors and their leadership strategies, professional trajectories, and advice for both other higher education leaders as well as aspiring leaders. All ten authors from the previous publication and thirteen additional authors for this volume are IAUP members who have transformed not only their own campuses but also global higher education.

We are most thankful for the work led by Dr. Lieberman, and we extend our appreciation to each of the authors of the 2024 and 2026 publications, who contributed inspirational and visionary thoughts and wisdom.

Information about this volume and the 2024 publication will be available on IAUP's website.

On behalf of IAUP, I offer our deep admiration and sincere appreciation to Santander Universidades—and specifically to Arturo Cherbowski, executive director of Santander Universidades México, and director general of Universia México—for their generous support of our organization and this publication.

Our intention is that these companion publications will raise awareness, identify best practices, and share important lessons that will assist others who are already in leadership positions, as well as those who are embarking on senior leadership positions.

IAUP continues to support initiatives and global meetings that further the mission and vision of the organization while adding to the success of each member, president, and institution.

With profound appreciation,

Dr. Shawn Chen

President, IAUP 2024–27

President, Sias University (China)

Introduction: A Global Study of Gender and Presidential Leadership in Higher Education

Devorah Lieberman

Senior Consultant, International Association of University Presidents, and President Emerita, University of La Verne (United States)

The International Association of University Presidents: History, Mission, and Purpose

The International Association of University Presidents (IAUP)[1] has a rich history and a significant global mission. This chapter provides an overview of IAUP's distinctive origins, core objectives, and enduring relevance to higher education leadership across the world and serves as the introduction to the 2026 IAUP publication.

History

Founded in 1964 by university leaders from the United States, Puerto Rico, South Korea, the Republic of the Philippines, and Liberia, IAUP was created to facilitate international dialogue among university presidents as well as to foster personal connections and professional collaborations (IAUP 2025). To this day, IAUP remains a unique organization—likely the only global higher education association devoted exclusively to supporting collaboration and interaction among university presidents, rectors, and chancellors.

The inaugural IAUP conference took place in Oxford, England, in June 1965 and drew approximately 120 representatives from twenty-one countries. Since then, IAUP has grown to encompass hundreds of members across nearly 100 nations (IAUP 2025). Its academic events, global partnerships, and initiatives have earned the attention and respect of world leaders, scholars, and media alike. More information about IAUP is available through its website: www.iaup.org.

Mission and Purpose

IAUP's core mission is to strengthen the international dimension and overall quality of education at its member institutions. This is accomplished by

[1]THE INTERNATIONAL ASSOCIATION OF UNIVERSITY PRESIDENTS (IAUP) is an association of university chief executives from higher education institutions around the world. Membership is limited to those individuals who serve as presidents, rectors, or vice-chancellors at regionally accredited colleges or universities. Its primary purpose is to strengthen the international mission and quality of education of institutions in an increasingly interdependent world, and to promote global awareness and competence as well as peace and international understanding through education. For more information, visit www.iaup.org

fostering global awareness, cross-cultural competence, peace, and mutual understanding through education.

To achieve this, IAUP:

1. Maintains independence from ideological and political interests
2. Promotes dialogue, tolerance, justice, and peace on a global scale
3. Provides an active global network and forum for university presidents to:
    - Share their experiences and insights
    - Support universities in economically underserved regions
    - Broaden access for students from marginalized backgrounds
    - Advance qualitative development across higher education
    - Reinforce cultural diversity, which is essential to personal identity, social cohesion, and creativity

The Origin of This Initiative and the Two Companion Publications (2024 and 2026)

In line with IAUP's mission, Dr. Fernando León García—then president of IAUP and president of CETYS University (Mexico)—initiated in the summer of 2023 a new project to support and highlight the leadership of international women university presidents, rectors, and chancellors. The goal was twofold: to identify the transformative leadership attributes of women institutional leaders as well as to provide inspiration and guidance to mid-level administrators aspiring to these roles.

This led to IAUP's 2024 publication, *Spotlighting Female Leadership: Strategies, Stories, Perspectives* (Lieberman, 2024). The initiative had long been encouraged by IAUP members, including Dr. Gülsün Sağlamer, former rector of Istanbul Technical University; Dr. Elizabeth J. Stroble, chancellor of Webster University; and several other committed leaders.

As a longtime IAUP member and former president of the University of La Verne (2011–23), I was honored to assume the coordinating role in this effort after my retirement in August 2023. The first initiative, which resulted in the 2024 publication, now includes this companion volume for 2026 and broadens the conversation by engaging male presidents and chancellors as contributors. Both volumes seek to document and share effective leadership strategies for transformative outcomes and to suggest how both men and women leaders can advance professional pathways for others in higher education.

Goals of the 2024 Initiative

This initiative was designed to:

1. Identify strategic leadership skills demonstrated by women presidents worldwide
2. Examine how these women presidents globally can foster professional opportunities for women aspiring to top-level leadership roles
3. Result in a publication that focuses on both items one and two

Goals of the 2026 Initiative

This initiative was designed to:

1. Identify strategic leadership skills demonstrated by men presidents globally
2. Identify the themes that emerged from the 2024 women presidents, compared with those of the 2026 men presidents
3. Examine how both men and women presidents foster professional opportunities for people to ascend to the presidency
4. Result in a publication that focuses on items one through three

Overview of the 2024 Publication

The 2024 volume, *Spotlighting Female Leadership: Strategies, Stories, Perspectives*, features ten women university presidents, each from an IAUP member institution. The authors represent diverse countries, including the Kingdom of Spain, the Republic of Lithuania, the Republic of Türkiye, the United Mexican States, South Korea, the People's Republic of Bangladesh, and the United States of America.

Despite significant differences in geography, institution type, and culture, striking commonalities emerged among these female leaders. Each contributed a chapter structured around the following topics:

- Institutional overview
- Length of tenure
- Professional trajectory
- Gender and leadership
- Leadership strategies
- Advice for current women leaders
- Guidance for aspiring women leaders

Emergent Themes from the 2024 Volume

- First woman leader: Many reflected on being the first woman to lead their institution.
- Higher purpose: Many shared a sense of mission beyond self to serve students, institutions, and society.
- Mentorship: Many discussed the importance of mentors and coaches for support and growth.
- Listening: Many emphasized having humility, listening to others, and learning continually.
- Proving oneself: Many mentioned the need to overcome skepticism and gender bias.
- External perceptions: Many mentioned the impact of gender, age, nationality, and religion on how they as leaders are perceived.
- Key leadership attributes: Many shared essential attributes, including authenticity, empathy, resilience, focus, and humility.
- Imposter syndrome: Many shared their struggles with self-doubt and how they overcame it.
- Ascendancy: Many shared that their ascendancy was not traditional and was often encouraged by others.

Overview of the 2026 Publication

This 2026 volume expands the lens of the prior book by spotlighting thirteen transformative men presidents, rectors, and chancellors—all IAUP members—from institutions across the Commonwealth of Australia, Bangladesh, the People's Republic of China, the Republic of Colombia, Ecuador, Georgia, Japan, Mexico, the Kingdom of Morocco, the Republic of South Africa, Spain, the UK, and the US. These institutions range from small to large, public to private, and nonprofit to for-profit.

Each chapter addresses these topics:

- Institutional introduction
- Leadership tenure
- Professional journey
- Leadership contributions
- Personal identity and perception
- Advice to fellow leaders
- Guidance for aspiring leaders
- Strategies for professional ascendancy

Emergent and Comparative Themes Across the 2024 and 2026 Publications

- Mentorship and opportunity creation: Authors from both publications emphasized the value of mentorship and coaching. Women were more explicit than men in discussing their mentors; men described how they were supported and, in turn, how they actively created opportunities for others, especially women and underrepresented groups.
- Greater purpose: Authors from both publications described their leadership as purpose-driven, with commitment to improving their respective institutions, access for students, and positive employment outcomes, particularly for underserved populations.
- Leadership attributes: Authors from both publications shared their views on the necessary core qualities for effective leadership. These included authenticity, humility, communication, resilience, and empathy. Male leaders also emphasized patience, emotional intelligence, integrity, and perseverance.
- Paths to the presidency: The women leaders noted that their paths to the presidency were often nonlinear, with others observing leadership potential in them before they did. Men leaders also had diverse paths, but their narratives lacked the same emphasis on external validation, external encouragement, and instead emphasized internal locus of control.
- Communication and collaboration: Authors from both volumes highlighted the importance of inclusive communication, collaboration, and active listening to build trust and drive transformative change.

- *I* versus *we* language: The women authors generally used collective language that emphasized institutional accomplishments. Men authors tended to use more individual language that focused on personal contributions and vision.
- Proving oneself and facing imposter syndrome: The women authors often described the need to prove their worth and referenced succumbing to the imposter syndrome. These themes were absent from the men leaders' narratives, which focused more on strategic visioning and gaining campus trust.
- Earned versus privileged leadership: All twenty-three authors from both publications described their ascendancy to the presidency as being earned through demonstrated success rather than being inherited or expected. Regardless of socioeconomic or familial background, the most successful leaders in both volumes emphasized the importance of embodying principled leadership, with humility, authenticity, and commitment to mission. However, the male leaders often saw a presidency as part of their destiny or path, while the female leaders saw this more as an opportunity, not their destiny.

Conclusion: Leadership Roles and Responsibilities

As leaders of higher education institutions around the world, we must each recognize the power and responsibility inherent in our roles. Leadership is defined not by title alone but rather by a dedication to purpose, an unwavering commitment to equity, and an ability to elevate others while moving our institutions—and society—forward.

References

IAUP (International Association of University Presidents). 2025. "The History of IAUP." About IAUP. Accessed September 9, 2025. https://www.iaup.org/about-iaup/history/.

Lieberman, Devorah. 2024. *Spotlighting Female Leadership: Strategies, Stories, Perspectives*. International Association of University Presidents (IAUP). https://iaup.org/spotlighting-female-leadership-strategies-stories-perspectives.iaup/.

1 Leading with Purpose, Focusing on Performance

Amine Bensaid

President, Al Akhawayn University (Morocco)

Introducing My Institution: A Five-Year Journey of Transformation for a Bigger, Better and More Sustainable University

Nestled in the Middle Atlas Mountains of Morocco, Al Akhawayn University in Ifrane (AUI) embodies the remarkable vision of Hassan II, the late king of Morocco, and the spirit of mutual understanding and brotherhood he envisioned—a brotherhood relationship that two humans can share without being biological siblings.

The university was named *al akhawayn*, which in Arabic means "the two brothers," in reference to its two founders—King Hassan II of Morocco and the late King Fahd of Saudi Arabia—who enjoyed such a relationship.

They established the university to foster this kind of relationship between people of different cultures and civilizations—especially between people from the Arab and Muslim traditions, on the one hand, and people from other civilizations, on the other. This mission was incorporated into the 1993 Royal Dahir (decree), which constituted the founding charter of AUI. The university opened its doors in 1995 (AUI 2024).

To nurture this openness that is married with identity, AUI adopted the liberal arts and sciences model of education, as the foundation for all its majors (including engineering and business majors), established English as the language of instruction, and required proficiency in both Arabic and French. Over a third of AUI faculty are international citizens, and about half of AUI's graduates spend a semester or two on international exchange programs during their AUI journey (AAICU 2024). Rooted in a rich, multilayered cultural setting, AUI brings together local and global perspectives, fostering a dynamic academic environment that encourages critical thinking, ethical leadership, and innovation.

AUI has developed into a unique space in Morocco in which intellectual curiosity meets real-world impact. We are committed to offering a transformational college experience that shapes graduates who are equipped to pursue fulfilled lives as skilled professionals and engaged citizens—individuals who think independently, work interdependently, act responsibly, and contribute meaningfully to society.

AUI's approach blends rigorous academic training with a strong emphasis on civic engagement and experiential learning, preparing students to transition to society and to navigate a changing and increasingly interconnected world with both competence and purpose. AUI is accredited by the New England Commission of Higher Education (NECHE); it is the only US-accredited university in Morocco and one of only three US-accredited universities in Africa.

Championing Diversity and Advancement

AUI's commitment to inclusivity is reflected in its focus on community engagement, its diverse student body, and its leadership team. Fifty-four percent of its students are women, who also constitute 65 to 70 percent of the President's List (which recognizes students who have received the highest grades each semester). Further, two out of our three deans are women, and so is our director of human resources and our chief employability and entrepreneurship officer.

More than half of AUI's students receive scholarships or financial aid, and 48 percent are first-generation college students—underscoring the university's role as a social elevator. More than twenty years ago, AUI created its Azrou Center for Community Development, located about a thirty-minute drive from campus. It focuses on aiding the underserved local population, especially in the areas of women's health, capacity building, and entrepreneurship; supporting elementary and middle school non-completers to be reinserted in the school system; and training unemployed college graduates to develop skills and find jobs. The center has served 88,496 beneficiaries—62 percent of whom are women—and has achieved an employment rate of 71 percent.

Leadership Tenure

When I assumed the presidency of AUI in November 2019, I was fortunate to inherit an institution rich in history and solid in its foundations. Still, in a rapidly changing landscape, the university was also facing formidable challenges. In February 2020, we presented to our board a bold, strategic plan to grow the university from 1,900 to 5,000 students in five years; boost return on investment through innovations in our approach to career success; and partner with Gen Z students to learn together and measurably improve their well-being and readiness for leading fulfilled lives.

In March 2020, the Covid-19 pandemic struck, compelling swift and focused action to ensure community safety and student success. We sent students home, fundraised to support vulnerable families (both of those of our students as well as families in Ifrane), transitioned rapidly to online instruction, and catered to our international student population on campus.

We were the first university in Morocco to resume face-to-face classes in the fall of 2021, balancing safety with educational quality. In addition, and just as importantly, we had to decide what to do about our ambitious strategic objectives. We decided to pursue them without any change, in spite of the pandemic.

The journey has been marked by a deliberate, phased transformation of our institution. With an inspiring vision, it was clear that our ability to execute was going to be key. We created a new chief operating officer position and hired a seasoned leader; we created new academic leadership positions to support the Office of the Vice President for Academic Affairs, and we were fortunate to be joined by inspired faculty who knew the institution very well and shared a strong passion for making a difference. Our initial focus was on student success—setting up an online quality management system to support online instruction quality; revamping processes; restructuring support teams; and launching initiatives that prioritized mental, physical, and emotional well-being.

We created the new Office of Employability and Entrepreneurship, with a mission to boost experiential learning, enhance student job readiness, foster an entrepreneurial mindset, and serve as a recruitment agency for our partner employers.

We also instituted the new Office of Academic Support and Progress to advance student success and minimize the time a student needs to graduate—hence serving return on investment upstream. In parallel, we worked with the Academic Council (our elected faculty body that serves as the primary instrument of shared governance at AUI) to adapt our faculty appraisal policy according to these priorities.

Next, we expanded our academic offerings by developing undergraduate programs in renewable energy, territorial planning and management, environmental studies and sustainability, artificial intelligence (AI) and robotics, cloud and mobile software engineering, and big data analytics. We also secured funding for campus expansion and contracted with the government to promote inclusive access to AUI for students and families of diverse socioeconomic profiles.

Four years later, we have nineteen new buildings; twice the number of full-time faculty; over 4,000 students on campus; an 85 percent student satisfaction rate; a 92 percent retention rate; 48 percent first-generation students; and 84 percent of job-seeking graduates land at least one job offer before the end of their final academic year, with nearly one in five graduating students choosing to apply to graduate school.

Today, nearly half of all graduating students have had a chance to experience an international exchange (for at least one semester). In addition, while we have proficiency requirements in three languages, AUI students can choose electives from six different languages (up from only two in 2019). Each year, a number of students graduating from AUI earn admission to some of the most competitive graduate programs in the world—at institutions such as the University of Oxford, the University of Cambridge, Harvard University, Columbia University in the City of New York, New York University, HEC Paris, ESSEC Business School, and others—and last year one of our graduating students won a Rhodes Scholarship (a first for the graduate of any Moroccan university) and the year before one of our students won a prestigious McCall MacBain International Fellowship to McGill University (another first for Morocco).

In the meantime, we have also earned a ten-year institutional reaccreditation from NECHE and from the Commission on English program Accreditation for our Language Center, as well as program reaccreditations from ABET (formerly, the Accreditation Board for Engineering and Technology, Inc.), and from the European Foundation for Management Development.

We have also balanced AUI's budget for the first time in its history, and we're ranked as first among Moroccan universities in top-of-mind awareness and in consideration among students and parents.

Regionally, we engaged with our local community by supporting the city of Ifrane in developing its strategic roadmap, promoting impact research among our faculty to address local challenges, increasing public-sector continuing education (about tenfold), and supporting our student humanitarian clubs (whose actions benefit more than 16,000 people per year). Globally, we have forged new pathways into sub-Saharan Africa and China.

Our new ambition for AUI in its next five-year plan is to boost the role of liberal arts and sciences education in a technology-driven world. During an era in which machines are becoming better machines, we seek to master technology and use it to make humans better humans.

We will put AI and technology at the service of a liberal arts and sciences education to make it more scalable and adaptive, and we will uphold the humanities and social sciences as essential disciplines that shape ethical leadership, foster cultural literacy, and develop the ability to navigate complexity. We will also continue to grow our experiential learning programs to equip our students with the skills they need to add value to their organizations.

Professional Journey

My own leadership journey is deeply intertwined with AUI's history. Having joined the institution as a young assistant professor at the end of 1994—two months before AUI opened its doors to students for the first time—I lived through the start-up phase of AUI, with almost the entire system needing to be built from scratch.

The initial faculty of the School of Science and Engineering consisted of only eight professors. For the first few weeks, as the campus had not yet been delivered, we all shared one office and we gathered for dinner every night. As you can imagine, I've made many lifelong friends among the first cohort of AUI faculty, students, and staff. I have since served in various roles—faculty member, program coordinator, dean of engineering, and vice president for academic affairs and research. It is at AUI that I—a computer scientist and an AI researcher—came to appreciate liberal arts and sciences education and to become deeply committed to it. It is also at AUI that I actually learned firsthand how much of a melting pot Morocco is and has been.

As you can realize, I have developed a deep emotional connection to the university, to my faculty colleagues, to our support staff, and to my former students and other AUI alumni. It was during this period that I developed my passion for students. They're truly endearing, constantly endeavoring to protect "their AUI" from our mistakes. I cherish being with our students, but I'm not always sure how they feel about this president, "who can have ideas from the twentieth century"—as one student reflected during one of our meetings!

Through my tenure at AUI, I have developed a comprehensive understanding of the institution's inner workings. It is also at AUI that I've been confronted with making the difficult decision to move my focus from teaching and research to university leadership and management. After being offered a deanship in 1999, I resisted it for two years because I could not see myself as doing anything other than teaching and research. Eventually, I gave in to the argument that it was an opportunity to have more impact through systemic measures and faculty support. In hindsight, I believe this turned out to be correct.

On the other hand, I didn't imagine that this work could be thankless. I now believe that to be both resilient and fulfilled in a university leadership job, it's crucial to have a deep inner passion for impact and the courage to do the right thing—combined with the humility to stand corrected when one makes mistakes. I'm very grateful that I've been very blessed by both passion and courage for this job, and I continue my journey as a student of humility and vulnerability!

Prior to returning to AUI in 2019 after a long absence, I spent eight years as president of a private university in Casablanca, which I led through a merger and acquisition process that had become necessary in order to survive significant market shifts caused by regulatory changes and the advent of new competitors with significantly greater resources.

This existential experience was extremely humbling to me, and it was a turning point in my mindset. I discovered that academic quality and the purest intentions alone were not enough for an academic institution to not only survive but also thrive. I've also learned the hard way about markets and finance, as well as the importance of being less intellectual, more entrepreneurial, and more action-oriented in decision-making. I was also fortunate to work with and observe some leaders who've become role models for me.

I've witnessed the miracles that entrepreneurial grit can accomplish. This experience honed my leadership and management skills. It deepened my appreciation for the delicate balance between academic quality and financial sustainability as well as between tradition and innovation (or, simply, the need for change). These experiences collectively shaped my approach to leadership, which is pragmatic and results-driven but also values-based and rooted in a deep respect for institutional culture.

Distinct Contributions to Leadership

I believe that what sets my leadership apart from others is a fusion of private-sector efficiency with public-sector purpose. I've remained fundamentally an academic—a proud academic—who has grown aware, willing, and able to address market and financial issues and who no longer feels apologetic about it.

My anchor in this significant transformation (which I assume must be difficult for a majority of academics) has been a nonnegotiable commitment to my values and principles. At AUI, I've been very fortunate to have strong alignment with our board of trustees, as well as mutual trust with a critical mass of faculty.

I've led the implementation of a management-by-results approach, combining the rigor of market-driven practices with a profound belief in higher education's purpose and an understanding of its nuanced demands. This approach was pivotal to our success in doubling enrollment, achieving financial sustainability, attaining impressive inclusion and student employability, and securing a ten-year reaccreditation from NECHE alongside key programmatic accreditations. By fostering a culture of accountability and excellence, we redefined what AUI could achieve.

Effective Leadership Strategies

Vision and collaboration have been the cornerstones of our leadership strategy. The bottom-up development of two strategic plans (2020–25 and now 2025–30) provided clear roadmaps to balance ambitious strategic goals with actionable steps. Decision-making has been deliberately both inclusive and decisive. We have engaged the board of trustees, faculty, staff, and student leaders through shared governance structures.

Still, we also moved decisively to act with focus, as it is crucial to avoid becoming entangled in (often legitimate) intellectual challenges to equations that have no perfect solution. A relentless focus on our core key performance indicators (KPIs), including student recruitment and satisfaction and financial health and graduate employability, has been central to our strategy. The participative approach not only enhanced our decisions but also fostered a sense of collective ownership (or at least acceptance) by a vast majority.

Personal Identity and Perception

Leadership—to me—is a blend of purpose, passion, values, grit, pragmatism, and vulnerability. I am results-oriented, but I am also guided by my principles and values that emphasize authenticity and integrity as well as by my respect and empathy for human limitations. While I hold firm to my convictions, I remain a strong believer that others often have better ideas and am happy to adapt when new perspectives emerge. This balance of determination and flexibility has been essential in navigating the complexities of institutional change.

I view my team as both a source of strength and a humbling reminder of the interdependence that leadership entails. The commitment, integrity, and resilience of my team members have been instrumental in transforming strategic visions into reality, and I am profoundly grateful for their partnership.

Advice for Fellow Leaders

I'm profoundly humbled by the prospect of offering advice. I'm not sure that I have any universal answers or how I can extrapolate from my own experience. However, based on my experience, I can share my belief that college presidency is a highly demanding job with enormous potential for impact and fulfillment.

I believe it's critical not to manage it as a popularity contest. Rather, performance, impact, and even resilience will result from passion and purpose when combined with a values-based compass, a cohesive team, and a firm belief in collective intelligence.

Focus, action, and grit—with enough sense of vulnerability in order to adjust or correct whenever appropriate—are also critical to success. In my case, knowledge and love for my university as well as personally knowing a critical mass of faculty colleagues well enough to earn mutual trust have been precious assets.

Last but not least, I have found invaluable support in interacting with fellow presidents of other peer universities, and most of my better ideas—and ambitious dreams—have come from them!

Guidance for Aspiring Leaders

If you're like me, you may really appreciate not having to seek university leadership but being offered such privilege. In my case, I believe this came as a result of simply following my passion (long before I got into university leadership and without that even being a consideration in my mind), which itself was instrumental in building a track record that others have identified as useful for university leadership.

After I finally accepted shifting my focus from teaching and research to university leadership, the single most important challenge—and opportunity for improvement—I've faced has been to shift from a subject matter expert mindset to a growth mindset. With the latter, I'm more oriented to better understand myself, my relationship with others, and my wider environment; I'm drawn to investigating alternative perspectives and different truths and to challenging the status quo; and I learn to own my inevitable shortcomings while turning to others for help and new ideas—all and always in pursuit of the university's vision as the critical North Star.

In my first presidency, I learned the hard way that academic quality is necessary but not sufficient for a university to survive and thrive. Market and finance acumen, as well as a capable president's team, are just as important. Finally, I believe that because I find a rewarding personal sense of purpose in my presidency, the opportunity cost associated with it is worthwhile.

References

AAICU (Association of American International Colleges & Universities). 2024. "Al Akhawayn University in Ifrane (AUI)." https://www.aaicu.org/al-akhawayn-university-in-ifrane-aui/.

AUI (Al Akhawayn University in Ifrane). 2024. "About AUI." Accessed September 9, 2025. https://aui.ma/about-aui.

2 Creating a Better and Brighter Future

Tim Brailsford

President and Vice Chancellor, Bond University (Australia)

Bond University, founded in 1989, is Australia's first private, independent, and nonprofit university. The university's mission is to provide an exceptional and life-changing student experience.

The university welcomed the first cohort of 322 students to its brand new, state-of-the-art campus on the Gold Coast on Australia's eastern seaboard, otherwise best known for its famous beaches and tourism opportunities.

When those foundation students graduated, they were quickly recruited by Australia's most successful corporations and their subsequent achievements in the workplace firmly established Bond's reputation for excellence.

Bond's vision was to offer an exclusive educational experience of the highest international academic standards through which students from around the world would be mentored in small classes by renowned academics with access to captains of business and industry.

Bond University has since become one of Australia's leading tertiary institutions, renowned for its expertise in professionally oriented disciplines in business, law, medicine, architecture, screen and media, psychology, and sports-related fields. New disciplines have been introduced in actuarial science, data analytics, and allied health.

Bond has been consistently and independently ranked as Australia's number one university for student experience for almost two decades. Further, employers report that they are more satisfied with Bond graduates than those from any other university.

Bond's achievements have exceeded the expectations of many, meeting every challenge with the unbridled spirit of determination and innovation that has characterized its rich and colorful but relatively young history.

Our university's method for success is simple: we set out to be deliberately different from every other university in Australia. The majority of programs are delivered in person, with a student-staff ratio of 11:1. Degrees are delivered over trimesters, providing our students with a personal, high-quality, carefully curated educational experience that waves farewell to graduates who are primed and ready to walk into their career of choice. We proudly welcome students from all corners of the globe who make their new home at Bond University and make our student body a diverse and enlightened society of perspectives, insights, and experiences.

We are home to an elite sporting program that consistently features proud Olympians. These student-athletes choose Bond University for a specific reason—we tailor delivery of their studies around their high-performance sporting careers, making it possible for these impressive students to achieve the very best in their athletic endeavors while simultaneously undertaking their academic pursuits.

Our students' experiences do not stop once they graduate. Life as a Bondy is not a fleeting or temporary experience. "Once a Bondy, always a Bondy" is a mantra amongst staff, students, and alumni alike.

Leadership Tenure

At the time of writing, I have been in the role of president at my current institution for more than thirteen years. I have seen my tenure broadly through the lens of subperiods of around five years each.

New initiatives and changes take time to embed in higher education institutions. Universities are places of rich tradition that is held dear by academic staff, students, and alumni. This is a strength in providing the bedrock of a university's mission, values, and culture. However, all institutions need to adapt and move forward.

My first five years as president were spent embedding core values, elements of which were in place due to the hard work of my predecessors. Bond University is a relatively young institution, and it was important to implement a whole-campus approach to key aspects of our mission.

My second five years capitalized on our positioning and previous efforts, which resulted in substantial expansion of programs, student cohorts, and infrastructure. This was also a period during which significant advancement and brand recognition were achieved. However, as will be discussed, the latter part of this period coincided with the advent of the global Covid-19 pandemic.

The current subperiod might be best characterized by an era of innovation and renewal—partly in response to external forces but also in reflection of a determination to embrace continuous improvement.

During my overall tenure, there has been dramatic technological advancement, most recently including the development of generative artificial intelligence. We have also witnessed substantial shifts in student sentiment and stakeholder expectations, volatility in geopolitical forces and global relations, swings in global and national economies, and unprecedented changes in government higher education policies and priorities, and—of course—a global pandemic. The ability to respond to these forces with dexterity has never been more crucial to ensure the future success of the institution.

There is little doubt that the global pandemic—which lasted for two years and left an aftermath that drifted on for several more years—was an extraordinary moment for my institution and, arguably, for every educational institution. In short, it was a defining moment for all leaders of education.

In Australia, the restrictions imposed by the government during the pandemic were particularly stringent by global standards. For two years, inbound and outbound international travel was effectively prohibited in all but exceptional circumstances. Moreover, domestic travel was severely affected due to the introduction of bans on border crossings between states and provinces. These restrictions were particularly problematic for our university, which is located close to a provincial border that is crossed on a regular basis by many of our students and staff for study, work, and daily life.

Bond University's student body is highly diverse and can be broadly categorized by three cohorts. Around one-third of students are drawn from the local region, another third originate from other domestic regions that involve at least 1,000 kilometers of travel, and the remaining third arrive from overseas. Thus, around two-thirds of the student population leave their homes to live and study at the university.

When the pandemic arrived, these students were faced with the choice of returning home, staying on campus, or relocating nearby for an unknown period. Understandably, many students returned home. This had a profound effect on how we subsequently taught and engaged with our student and staff community.

As many educational institutions did, we moved to a world of online teaching and learning. Our challenge, while not unique, was to balance the demands and expectations of students who had decided to stay on campus in order to have a normal university experience with those of students who were located remotely and expected a high-quality virtual experience. It was difficult and compounded by an increasingly tight fiscal environment as we struggled to replace graduating students with new student enrollments severely hampered by travel restrictions with no end in sight.

We formed the Innovation Task Force in response to the challenges of the pandemic with membership drawn from all over campus. The task force's role was to come up with new ideas and innovations that would shape the future. No idea was regarded as crazy, and we broke the shackles of tradition. That task force became the engine room for effective change—much of which is still in place today.

While I was confident that we would manage to successfully navigate our way through the chaos of the pandemic, there were daily concerns raised by colleagues. During that time—as the weeks turned into months and the months turned into years—we certainly experienced moments of doubt. However, we stood steadfast and emerged post-pandemic as a more tight-knit community, with a strong sense of self-belief and pride.

The lessons from that period have been well learned; the power of innovation was brought about by crisis, and those innovations are serving our university well to this day.

Professional Journey

From a personal perspective, I have been exceedingly fortunate to benefit from exceptional academic supervisors during my studies early in life and, subsequently, during my professional career. Their direction and wisdom gave me much-needed insight into the world of academia.

Ours is a unique industry that is heavily dependent on people and their interactions. These interactions may be in a classroom, a research laboratory, a field trip, a committee meeting, an international conference, or through membership of various national and international associations. Yet each interaction makes a positive impact on our community and is an opportunity for individuals to learn and grow.

Some of these interactions can be more impactful than others. In my personal case, at a relatively early stage of my career, I became involved with a prestigious international accreditation system that involved peer reviews and benchmarking. I am still involved with this body, some thirty years later. Through this engagement, I learned about the diversity of international systems, different frameworks, environmental settings, traditions, and cultures. For instance, these experiences included the European Bologna Process, the UK system of quality assurance, the US tradition of academic tenure, the governance complexity across provinces such as in India, the

French culture of industry collaboration, and the German focus on research partnerships.

These experiences enabled me to share international perspectives with my own institution in Australia. Each system held valuable and unique attributes that the people inside the system take for granted, but it is consistently remarkable how some of these features have not been translated into international practice. Hence, my personal approaches to strategy, management, and innovation are informed by observations from around the globe.

I have also benefited from strong engagement with other sectors and industries. University systems can be internally focused, but we do not have the advantage of seeing ourselves as others do. This is particularly relevant when designing curricula, launching new research programs, and remaining at the forefront of new developments.

A strong and engaged industry advisory board, both at the institutional level and across the various academic schools within a university, can provide forums for vibrant, energetic, and influential discussion. New, original ideas and strategies can be proposed and informed by listening to the advice of those who are on the outside looking in.

Distinct Contributions to Leadership

Prior to the role I occupy, my experience in academic institutions was heavily focused on research activities. While the teaching of students was also a central role, my performance metrics were heavily weighted in research outcomes and achievements.

I had often pondered whether the emphasis on research had gone too far and if the interests of students were left as a mere afterthought. During discussions held through the recruitment process for my current role as a university president, it was clear that a unique approach was required at Bond University. Moreover, our distinctive positioning needed to be more effectively promoted and used as a platform to align and coordinate a range of strategic plans.

For a variety of reasons, I believed my new institution was in an excellent position to lead innovation and best practices in learning, teaching, and student success. As a result, the motto that students come first was instilled in our academic and professional staff. This motto effectively served as a call to arms across the institution to accentuate our efforts in student engagement and view their personal successes as institutional successes. This approach enabled reforms in the curriculum, teaching methods, implementation of a range of cocurricular activities and opportunities, investment in student support mechanisms, and rollout of a series of positive interventions designed to underpin the student lifecycle from enrollment through graduation and beyond.

Importantly, this approach was embraced by the student body, which quickly realized that the university was its partner and there to guide and assist them on their educational journey. While nothing in this approach was particularly radical, the whole-institution focus and the continual development of improvement initiatives led to the adoption of a culture that evolved from the grass roots of the university; thus, it has become entrenched as part of our identity.

The spin-off benefits—such as the natural development of a strong brand and value proposition that puts students at the center and avoids the crowded space of global rankings and hollow claims of being "world class"—became infectious. We had developed a brand that was authentic, and our graduates were happy to be proud ambassadors and provide strong testimonials. Moreover, our nonteaching staff, such as those in support roles and administration, also became invested in student success. This created a united and shared purpose across all areas of campus.

Effective Leadership Strategies

"The task of the leader is to get their people from where they are to where they have not been."—Henry Kissinger

Kissinger's wisdom is simple in its structure yet deep in meaning. Change is hard, and effective change is a constant battle that can seem to be never-ending. At their cores, universities are centered on humans and their interactions with each other, society, and the world around them. Leaders need to be prepared and ready to lead change.

History is littered with case studies of institutional malaise and decline, whereby ex post analysis reveals critical junctures at which decisions were either not taken or were taken poorly—think of the Kodak moment.

People tire of constant change, however, and morale can decline when change fatigue sets in. Somewhere on this continuum, there is a delicate balance between ensuring that institutions can adapt and be ready for the future, whilst not creating an environment that is full of perpetual uncertainty and the appearance of chaos.

Every institution will undergo change, driven by either internal forces or external influences, and often a combination of both. People need to be led on a journey of change, and communication is critical in this regard.

Major change should never arrive as unexpected news. University communities are not immune from rumor and conspiracy theories. An effective change strategy is to communicate early and ensure that the most impacted stakeholders have the opportunity for input. Focus groups, discussion forums, and working parties are effective mechanisms to float ideas and ascertain pressure points.

In a world of multiple communication channels, it is important for a leader not to rely upon any single medium. Written communiques should be preceded by genuine consultation and discussion. Generally, communities will be receptive to change—even if they dislike it—provided they believe that they have been listened to and have had an opportunity to give feedback.

Thus, the establishment of a clear communication plan should be an essential step in any proposal for change. These can be difficult conversations, but there are long-term benefits. If there is difficult news to deliver, then the leader should deliver the message. Most institutional change should ultimately be focused on creating a better and brighter future. It is important to stay on message and ensure that other leaders within disciplines and portfolios share in this direction. Hence, the early engagement of sectional leaders is critical.

While the role of a president can be singled out, the reality is that no single individual can operate effectively in isolation. The president's role should be viewed as that of the team captain, whose responsibility is to engender trust and respect. A leader should regularly communicate with their team, both collectively and individually, and take the time to understand them as individuals; learning about their families, personal traits, and interests all assist in building that culture of trust and respect.

Personal Identity and Perception

University presidents may sometimes appear aloof and disconnected from their community. This is a common accusation expressed by critics and some in the media. Once this criticism receives airtime, it can spread quickly and embed itself as a more general perception.

The role of a president is complex and requires a different approach at different times to different stakeholders. It is a daily task—and, indeed, a daily duty—to engage with stakeholders. This may take many forms, such as speaking with students, attending faculty and staff meetings, calling donors and supporters, sending best wishes and flowers on special occasions, recognizing notable milestones, or being open to ad hoc requests for a coffee and chat.

The president needs to be seen as accessible and available. This can be challenging given the sheer volume of business and urgency of the administrative demands of the role, which leads to limited space in the calendar. However, it is essential to break down the perceived barriers between the executive management of an institution and those who perform critical functions in teaching and learning, research and innovation, and service delivery.

I believe that all stakeholders have a strong desire to be seen through the lens of individuality. Each person is different—with their own needs, wants, and peculiarities. Part of the role of a president is to create a variety of opportunities for stakeholders to engage with them.

Any appearance of personal goals or ambitions by senior leaders can be a recipe for disaster, as it might be interpreted that the leader is putting their personal agenda ahead of their community. Thus, a leader must be constantly wary of self-promotion. It is always better for someone else to speak in high regard of one's achievements and successes. Humility is a trait that others respect.

In this regard, it is important for a leader to praise others and not be drawn into personal comparisons. Academic faculty members have often sacrificed a lot in the pursuit of their passions. They typically become experts in their fields through an enormous dedication of their time, energy, and unswerving commitment to their passion and cause. They do not take kindly to those above who make comments or judgments about the value, relevance, or impact of their work or their discipline.

Advice for Fellow Leaders

There is an often-quoted observation that leadership can be lonely, which is sometimes attributed to Ferdinand Marcos, a former president of the Philippines. Regardless of its source, it is a truism. Very few decisions are ever celebrated by the whole. At best, one can hope that the majority supports one's judgment. There are other occasions in which you will feel certain that your decision will be disliked by the majority; however, it is a choice that must be made in the interests of the overall institution.

The hard decisions are made easier if you surround yourself with good people whose counsel is given without fear or favor. Decisions at the top are often not straightforward, else they would have been made by others before reaching the office of the president. Such decisions can be those that no one else wants to make. Hence, the outcome is likely to impact others and may not always be well received. In this regard, sage advice is critical.

Key sources of advice may come either formally or offline from the senior management team, such as the vice presidents and deans or the university's governing body. Whatever the source of the advice, it is valuable if it is impartial and honest and given with full regard to the institution's best interests. This means that discussions may sometimes be challenging, but a president must be prepared to listen and hear alternative points of view.

Early on in the appointment of a new leader, there is an initial period of grace—otherwise known as the honeymoon period—whereby the new leader is cut some slack. During this period, decisions are generally accepted notwithstanding their popularity or otherwise.

After a time, it is inevitable that the surge of goodwill wanes. It is at this stage that senior colleagues may find it difficult to stay fully aligned to their president, knowing that unpopular decisions will also reflect on themselves. These moments can be pivotal in defining the tenure of a leader. Presidents must be open to critical input and maintain a culture that values all opinions. Disagreements should never lead to an environment in which diverse views are dismissed or rejected out of hand.

In such times, diversity in its broadest form can be important and influential. We often see the call for diversity centered on color, race, ethnicity, or faith. Yet diversity of experience, knowledge, background, and—perhaps most of all—thought is especially valuable.

The foibles, nuances, and quirks of colleagues may occasionally become difficult to tolerate, but their presence should be welcome if they bring valuable contributions to the table that cause personal reflection. Every individual is different, and these differences should be encouraged and valued.

In a university setting, there is a complex myriad of stakeholders. Many universities are too large for the president to be closely involved across all of the stakeholder groups. The role of senior colleagues is crucial in keeping the president informed, as they will typically possess a greater in-depth knowledge of the relevant stakeholders within their respective portfolios. If a president is not receiving frank and fearless advice from their executive team, then steps must be taken to ensure that they can provide such guidance.

From personal experience, these junctures occur approximately three to five years into a tenure. Collegial friendships may become strained during this period, but it is the role of the lonely president to absorb this and respond accordingly.

Difficult times require courage, but there are many who have successfully walked the same path. Despite many differences across national and geopolitical boundaries, universities face similar challenges and circumstances. International networks such as IAUP can be effective conduits for a president to seek advice, solace, and mentorship without competitive forces or influences.

Guidance for Aspiring Leaders

Leadership is a privilege. Some say it must be earned, and that much is true. However, whatever the achievements, accomplishments, or reasons behind a leader's appointment, they must be parked at the door. For once an individual walks through that door, they must make an immediate transition. I suspect that anyone reading this will recall instances of individuals who failed to make this transition.

Prior to my appointment as president, I had served four terms as a faculty dean across two highly respected institutions. Each of these terms were served under different university presidents. Through these experiences, I was able to listen and learn from leaders with different styles, philosophies, and approaches to management and stakeholders. I also had the privilege of visiting many institutions overseas as an academic and during my time as a dean, during which I was fortunate to observe and learn from a wide variety of tertiary leaders.

An insight I gleaned is that there is no single perfect style or set of attributes that a successful president must possess. While there are some essential core skills and attributes required to succeed in the role, the reality is that different circumstances, different times, different stakeholders, and different challenges all require different approaches to leadership. What may work for one institution will not necessarily work for another institution. Similarly, what may work at a certain point in time will not necessarily work at another time.

While universities are sometimes painted as slow-moving entities that are hamstrung by tradition, the reality is far different. Academic institutions are generally at the forefront of change. The emergence of new knowledge, disciplines, technology, and even societal attitudes is typically associated with higher education. Universities are hotbeds of innovation and new thinking. In such an environment, university leaders must be prepared to embrace change and be receptive to new ideas.

The future is unknown, but that does not mean that we cannot be prepared. Arguably, universities are currently facing their greatest challenges in many decades and will do so for several years to come. Most of these challenges are driven by external forces which makes them even more difficult to resolve. Moreover, many of the challenges intersect—creating complexity and requiring multifaceted and multilayered solutions.

All of these considerations point to a critical need for those seeking leadership positions to be adaptive, flexible, and capable of change. Psychologists will debate whether individuals possess these attributes innately at birth or whether they can be learned; notwithstanding, my belief is that any individual can work on improving these attributes irrespective of their starting point.

Universities promote and encourage lifelong learning. While the focus of lifelong learning is typically on students and their future career path, it is equally applicable to those working in universities and particularly those holding key leadership positions. Learning is not restricted to formalized courses and programs with strong structures around them; rather, informal learning can be just as valuable—if not more. Opportunities for informal learning present themselves on a daily basis from observing others, reading widely, reflecting on history, and participating in discussion and debate on topics outside of one's comfort zone.

I would encourage anyone considering a leadership role to gain experience in different institutions under different leaders facing different challenges. Engage in as many informal learning opportunities that present themselves, and reflect on whether your personal behaviors, actions, and decisions would have been appropriate and successful in those situations. Learn from others' successes and failures, and understand why mistakes were made. Recognize that a leader is never correct all the time, but a successful leader is one who can adapt and adjust so that mistakes are not repeated and successes can be planned.

Championing Diversity and Advancement

There are many programs to assist institutions to achieve greater diversity and work toward addressing historical imbalances from underrepresented groups. Some of these programs are quite formalized and embedded within expectations of government, regulators, and accreditation agencies at both national and international levels. Other programs are offered by specialist organizations—often nonprofits—and take a softer approach designed to engineer long-lasting change. More programs can be found amongst a range of commercial suppliers in the human resources and training industries.

Many of these programs have strengths and potential to make a positive impact. However, importing any program from the outside is fraught with risk if there is not an appetite from internal stakeholders to undertake genuine change.

Cultural change is the best form of change as it spreads throughout an entire institution, and it can successfully override traditions and norms. However, changes in culture can be hard to achieve and may require several attempts. Quick wins can be reversed when they collide with entrenched views and attitudes.

External programs often specify metrics that are used to measure progress and develop reporting statistics. Such metrics typically boil down to simple measures such as participation and attainment, which miss the complexity of change. While measurement of progress is a highly desirable goal, it should not become a means of itself. For instance, appointment decisions still need to have a quality emphasis even though there may be an underlying desire to chase metrics.

At the least, external programs need to be supplemented by an internal program, and one that is led from the top. For change to last, it must become embedded in the psyche of the institution and its people.

One such program that I have observed to be quite successful is built around three pillars:

- Providing role models
- Creating opportunities
- Inspiring confidence

People love to be inspired, which in turn drives their own aspirations. We can all relate to examples from various walks of life in which we have seen someone else achieve the impossible and that has subsequently changed our dreams and ambitions. Hence, institutions need to recognize the importance of role models from minority groups and underrepresented populations.

Institutions can sometimes get caught up in viewing their world as full of binary decisions. However, within a university and particularly in the academic realm, there are a myriad of ways in which opportunities can be created through some innovative thinking. For instance, if someone shows promise but is not yet ready to step up to a leadership position, then why not give them some experience first through a part-time position or a short-term secondment? Review each vacancy as it arises and explore options as to how a vacancy could be filled with the objective of creating opportunity. Examine academic leadership roles to see if there is scope to create a deputy or assistant position through which someone could be trained to take over in due course. Establish a mentoring system that enables aspiring individuals to view their future career through the eyes of another.

Finally, it is important to create an environment that inspires confidence and enables individuals to feel comfortable in striving to realize ambition. For instance, it is widely held and supported by evidence that women take longer than men to apply for work-based promotion. In an academic setting, promotion is one of the key forms of leadership advancement. Thus, equipping good candidates for promotion with support is essential to bolstering their confidence.

This might include providing key pieces of information to allow them to fully understand the process, connecting them with individuals who have experienced the process, conducting mock interviews, and sourcing senior colleagues to assist with the preparation of their case. These are all relatively straightforward initiatives that can be introduced at minimal cost to inspire confidence.

3 Transforming Through Service-Driven Leadership

Sabur Khan

Founder and Chairman, Daffodil International University (Bangladesh)

Introducing My Institution

When I envisioned the foundation of Daffodil International University (DIU) back in 2002, I dreamed of creating more than just a university—I dreamed of building a transformative ecosystem where education, innovation, and values come together to prepare individuals to shape the future of our nation. Today, DIU stands as a leader in higher education in Bangladesh, blending academic excellence with innovation, values, and global connections. Our strength lies in 60,000 alumni spread across the globe, 51 diverse academic programs, 150 state-of-the-art labs, and more than 580 international initiatives that connect our students with the world.

Driven by the vision of Nobel Laureate Professor Muhammad Yunus, DIU is creating the world's first three-zero campus—zero carbon emissions, zero poverty, and zero unemployment. Through renewable energy, entrepreneurship, and social business initiatives led by DIU's Yunus Social Business Centre (YSBC), we empower students to build a sustainable and inclusive future. I will also add that YSBC embodies the spirit of change by fostering research, innovation, and initiatives that align with the three-zero vision.

Mission

DIU's mission is to contribute to national development by producing skilled, ethical, and visionary graduates. We aim to nurture critical thinkers, problem-solvers, and leaders who can address the challenges of the modern world and shape a brighter future.

Unique Attributes

- Focus on employability: Programs such as Employability 360 and microcredentialing ensure that graduates are prepared for both local and global careers.
- Entrepreneurship ecosystem: DIU fosters innovation and supports students in launching their own ventures, transforming them into creators rather than job seekers.
- Technology-driven education: With cutting-edge facilities and digital learning platforms, DIU ensures students stay ahead in a tech-driven era.
- Global outlook: Partnerships with over 100 universities worldwide and exchange programs provide students with unparalleled global exposure.

Current Priorities

- Enhancing quality: We focus on continuously improving programs and research to meet international standards.
- Fostering innovation: We encourage impactful research and creative solutions for societal challenges.
- Community responsibility: We promote sustainability and a culture of giving back.
- Expanding global reach: We aim to position DIU as a global hub for diverse learners and international collaborations.

Future Focus

At DIU, we believe education shapes the future. Our focus lies in nurturing not only skilled graduates but also responsible, value-driven citizens. Through initiatives such as Art of Living, we instill respect, empathy, and social responsibility—ensuring that students measure success by the positive impact they create.

Looking ahead, we are integrating advanced technologies, artificial intelligence, and global perspectives into our programs while upholding the human values at the core of education. Our mission is to inspire leaders, innovators, and changemakers who will shape a better tomorrow.

A Story of Transformation

DIU is more than a university—it's a movement for transformation. Every milestone we achieve reflects in the stories of students turning obstacles into opportunities, building businesses, excelling in careers, and leading with purpose.

Leadership Tenure

My Journey with DIU

When I reflect on my journey with DIU, which I founded in 2002, it feels like witnessing a dream taking shape over two decades. The journey has been one of facing challenges, demonstrating persistence, and maintaining an unwavering belief in the transformative power of education. From the very first day, my vision for DIU was to build an institution that would not only provide knowledge but also nurture leaders, innovators, and changemakers who could transform society.

The following have been defining moments during my leadership:

- Establishing DIU and witnessing its growth: Watching DIU grow from a small idea into a nationally and internationally recognized institution has been one of the most rewarding experiences of my life. From gaining prestigious accreditations to introducing forward-thinking programs, each milestone has been a step closer to realizing the vision of a university that stands as a beacon of quality and innovation.
- Pioneering information and communication technology (ICT) education: In the early 2000s, when ICT was still an emerging field in Bangladesh, I made it a priority to integrate it into DIU's core. Today, I take pride in seeing our students excel as skilled IT professionals who are making meaningful contributions locally and globally.
- Fostering entrepreneurship: One of my deepest passions is empowering young people to believe in their ideas. Through DIU's vibrant entrepreneurship ecosystem, we have supported countless student start-ups, created incubation centers, and nurtured the entrepreneurial mindset.
- Focus on employability: I firmly believe that education must prepare students for the realities of the professional world. Programs such as Employability 360 and microcredentialing have ensured that DIU graduates are not just academically prepared but are also career-ready and equipped with practical skills to thrive.
- Expanding international horizons: Building global partnerships has been another cornerstone of my leadership. DIU now collaborates with esteemed universities worldwide to provide opportunities for student and faculty exchanges, global learning experiences, and international exposure.
- Commitment to community: I have always believed that education must give back to society. DIU's community engagement initiatives reflect this philosophy and focus on sustainability, social responsibility, and empowering underprivileged communities.

Achievements and Challenges

Through these efforts, DIU has been recognized with numerous awards and accolades. Our students and alumni have become changemakers, and our faculty has driven impactful research and innovation. Yet the road has not been without its obstacles. Establishing and growing a private university in Bangladesh meant overcoming challenges such as resource limitations, shifting mindsets about education, and ensuring quality amidst rapid growth. But every challenge has taught me resilience and reaffirmed my belief in DIU's mission.

Looking Ahead

As I reflect, I see the faces of students who have transformed their lives through DIU. I see their businesses, their innovations, their impact on society—these stories are the true measure of DIU's success. Moving forward, my focus remains on integrating advanced technologies, fostering value-based education, and preparing our youth for global leadership.

This journey has been one of shared dreams and collective efforts, and I remain committed to building a brighter future—one student, one innovation, and one step at a time.

Professional Journey

Reflecting on My Journey: Building a Purpose-Driven Foundation

My journey into entrepreneurship and education has been shaped by a series of experiences and values that have guided me every step of the way. It is not a story of personal achievement but rather one of perspective, purpose, and enduring commitment to creating opportunities for others.

Early Influences: Shaping a Vision

From an early age, I was deeply influenced by the values of hard work, perseverance, and responsibility in service to the community. These principles were not just lessons but rather a way of life that was instilled in me through my upbringing. When I was growing up, I found myself drawn to technology—not just for what it was but also for what it could do. Technology represented to me the ability to break barriers, connect people, and solve problems that once seemed insurmountable.

With this vision in mind, I pursued studies in computer science and began to dream of a Bangladesh where technology could empower lives, bridge inequalities, and create a platform for new opportunities. The potential I saw in technology wasn't just about innovation; it was about its power to transform the lives of individuals and communities.

A Perspective on Purpose

This foundation of values and vision ultimately guided me to where I am today. For me, entrepreneurship and education are deeply connected—both are about creating opportunities, enabling individuals to realize their potential, and building systems that leave a lasting impact. As I reflect on this path, it's clear that every step has been driven by a purpose bigger than myself. It has always been about the belief that education and technology together hold the key to unlocking the future of our nation.

This perspective continues to shape my work and inspires me to push forward—not for recognition but rather for the change it can bring to the lives of others. I share this journey to encourage others to look forward toward a future in which innovation, education, and purpose come together to create a better tomorrow.

Entrepreneurial Beginnings: A Catalyst for Change

In 1990, I founded Daffodil Computers Ltd., one of the pioneering IT companies in Bangladesh. This entrepreneurial venture taught me invaluable lessons about innovation and business management as well as the critical importance of skilled human resources. It also revealed a pressing challenge in the lack of a skilled workforce in Bangladesh, particularly in ICT. This realization planted the seed of a deeper purpose—to bridge the gap through education.

A Leap into Education: Building DIU

In 2002, I took a transformative step by establishing Daffodil International University. My vision was clear: I sought to create a world-class institution that could prepare graduates to thrive in an interconnected and rapidly evolving world. My background in business deeply influenced DIU's approach, emphasizing practical skills, employability, and entrepreneurship. I wanted our graduates not only to excel academically but also to be job creators, problem-solvers, and changemakers.

Leadership and Global Contributions: Expanding Horizons

As chairman of DIU, I have had the privilege of steering its growth into one of Bangladesh's leading universities, with a strong focus on academic excellence, innovation, and social responsibility. Beyond DIU, my leadership roles, such as serving as president of the Association of Universities of Asia and the Pacific (AUAP) and the Dhaka Chamber of Commerce & Industry (DCCI), have broadened my perspective. These experiences have reinforced my belief in the power of collaboration and the critical role of education in driving national and global progress.

Key learnings along the way have involved:

- Vision and innovation: The ability to anticipate future needs and innovate accordingly has been crucial in navigating the complexities of higher education and technology.
- Empowerment and collaboration: Empowering individuals and fostering collaboration has unlocked immense potential in both education and industry.
- Social responsibility: I have always believed that educational institutions carry a moral obligation to contribute to societal development and address the challenges of our time.

A Journey of Purpose

What drives me most is witnessing transformation in the lives of young people. From students creating impactful start-ups to graduates leading global organizations, their stories fuel my commitment to education. My journey is not just about building an institution—it is about creating a platform for young minds to dream, innovate, and contribute meaningfully to society.

As I look ahead, I remain bold in my mission to empower the youth of Bangladesh and beyond. Through education, we can rewrite narratives, bridge divides, and create a future in which knowledge serves as the greatest equalizer. This is not just my story—it is the story of Daffodil International University and its enduring impact on society.

Distinct Contributions to Leadership

Leadership, to me, is about creating impact, inspiring others, and driving meaningful change. My journey of transitioning from entrepreneurship to education has allowed me to approach this role with a perspective rooted in innovation, practicality, and purpose. Here's how I believe I bring a unique dimension to leadership:

1. Taking an entrepreneurial approach to education: My entrepreneurial background has profoundly shaped my leadership style. From building Daffodil Computers to founding Daffodil International University, I have always prioritized bridging the gap between industry and academia. I see education not just as a theoretical endeavor but as a practical tool to solve real-world challenges. At DIU, this vision translates into a focus on employability through which students are equipped with practical skills and opportunities that prepare them for the ever-changing job market.
2. Championing visionary thinking and early adoption: Early in my journey, I recognized the transformative potential of ICT in reshaping education. This realization positioned DIU as a pioneer in integrating technology into teaching and learning, making our programs dynamic and future-ready. I continue to emphasize the importance of critical thinking, problem-solving, and adaptability—skills that I believe are essential for success in the twenty-first century.
3. Seeking holistic education beyond the classroom: For me, education is not confined to academic excellence. It's about nurturing individuals to be responsible, empathetic, and innovative contributors to society. At DIU, we focus on holistic development—students are encouraged to grow personally, professionally, and socially. Through programs that emphasize social responsibility, leadership, and entrepreneurship, we ensure that our graduates leave not just with degrees but also with the necessary skills and values to make a meaningful difference.
4. Driving community impact and sustainability: Education should extend beyond the campus walls. I've always championed the role of

DIU in addressing societal challenges—whether through community engagement, sustainable practices, or fostering a sense of responsibility among students and faculty. These initiatives aren't just actions; they're values deeply embedded in the culture of DIU.

5 Fostering global perspectives: In today's interconnected world, education must be global. Over the years, I've prioritized international collaborations, creating opportunities for DIU students to engage with diverse cultures and perspectives. This not only enhances their learning but also prepares them to thrive in a globalized workforce.

I believe leadership is not about following a preset path but about constantly adapting, innovating, and inspiring. Through these contributions, I strive to make education at DIU transformative—not just for individuals but also for society at large.

Effective Leadership Strategies

Leadership is an evolving practice that requires a balance of vision and adaptability, as well as the ability to inspire and empower others. At DIU, my approach to leadership has been shaped by a commitment to collaboration, innovation, and meaningful impact. The following are the strategies I have employed, which I believe can serve as valuable insights for others aspiring to lead successfully in dynamic and challenging environments:

1 Craft a shared vision and driving collective ownership.
- Communicating purpose: A clear and compelling vision is at the heart of any successful institution. I ensure that DIU's goals are communicated consistently to all stakeholders, from faculty and staff to students and alumni, emphasizing our shared mission to transform education and empower youth.
- Engaging stakeholders: Leadership is not about issuing directives; it's about creating buy-in. I involve faculty, students, and staff in decision-making processes by encouraging them to contribute ideas and feel ownership of the university's direction.
- Ensuring strategic alignment: Every initiative at DIU is aligned with our broader strategic vision. This ensures that individual efforts contribute to the collective purpose, which creates a sense of unity and focus.

2. Empower individuals to lead.
   - Decentralizing leadership: I believe leadership must extend beyond the leader. By delegating authority and trusting individuals, I empower others to take initiative and responsibility in their respective roles.
   - Creating professional growth opportunities: At DIU, we invest in our people by providing access to mentorship programs, training workshops, and leadership development opportunities that enable them to unlock their potential.
   - Recognizing achievements: Recognition is a powerful motivator. Whether celebrating faculty accomplishments or student milestones, acknowledging contributions builds confidence and fosters commitment.

3. Lead by example.
   - Setting the standard: Leadership begins with integrity, accountability, and consistency. I strive to embody these values in my actions, creating a standard for others to follow.
   - Inspiring through passion: My dedication to education and innovation is not just a role—it's a calling. This passion, I believe, inspires those around me to approach their own work with enthusiasm and purpose.
   - Fostering resilience and adaptability: During challenges, I prioritize demonstrating resilience and adaptability to show others the importance of staying grounded while navigating uncertainty.

4. Cultivate a culture of collaboration.
   - Breaking silos: Higher education thrives on interdisciplinary collaboration. I encourage departments to work together, bridge gaps, and foster innovation through collective efforts.
   - Encouraging transparent communication: Open dialogue is the cornerstone of trust. Whether through town halls, informal discussions, or structured feedback sessions, I ensure everyone feels heard and valued.
   - Building community: DIU is not just an institution; it's a community. By fostering connections among faculty, students, and alumni, we create a supportive ecosystem that thrives on mutual respect and shared purpose.

5 Drive innovation as a core value.
   - Encouraging experimentation: True progress comes from the willingness to take risks and embrace new ideas. I encourage faculty and students to push boundaries by fostering a culture of experimentation and creativity.
   - Promoting entrepreneurship: DIU has established itself as a hub for entrepreneurship, and it offers incubation programs, start-up resources, and mentorship to inspire the next generation of changemakers.
   - Leveraging technology: In an era of rapid technological advancement, I have prioritized the integration of ICT and emerging technologies into our teaching, research, and administration, keeping DIU ahead of the curve.

6 Commit to continuous improvement.
   - Undergoing institutional self-reflection: No institution is perfect, and I believe in regular self-assessment. By seeking feedback from stakeholders and benchmarking against global best practices, DIU remains dynamic and progressive.
   - Adapting to change: Education must evolve with the times. Whether addressing shifts in global industry demands or embracing new educational paradigms, I emphasize the importance of adaptability to remain relevant and impactful.
   - Pioneering sustainable practices: DIU recognizes the urgent need for environmental and social responsibility and integrates sustainability into its curriculum and operations, which contributes to a better future.

7 Inspire a global outlook with local relevance.
   - Nurturing international collaboration: I have tried to develop DIU's global partnerships by opening doors for exchange programs, collaborative research, and exposure to diverse perspectives.
   - Making local impact with global standards: While embracing a global outlook, I have tried to ensure that DIU remains deeply connected to addressing local challenges. This dual focus ensures that our students are both world-class professionals and contributors to national development.

Reflections on Leadership

To me, leadership transcends strategy—it is about building an ecosystem of trust, empowerment, and shared purpose. At DIU, I have focused on harmonizing innovation with tradition, integrating global perspectives with local priorities, and balancing ambition with accountability. True leadership lies in serving others, fostering collaboration, and nurturing growth to create transformative change.

This journey has reinforced a profound lesson: Leadership is not about the individual but rather the collective. It is about cultivating an environment in which every member feels valued for their contribution, is inspired by the mission, and remains committed to advancing a shared vision. When people are empowered, their collective potential drives extraordinary progress.

Personal Identity and Perception

The trajectory of my leadership as chairman of Daffodil International University has been shaped by profound elements of my identity and personal experiences. These aspects not only define my approach to leadership but also influence how others perceive and interact with me in this role:

1. Roots in rural Bangladesh: Growing up in rural Bangladesh gifted me with an intrinsic sense of empathy and understanding for the barriers many face, particularly in accessing quality education. These experiences serve as the cornerstone of my commitment to empowering underprivileged yet talented individuals through education. My background also keeps me grounded and ensures that my leadership reflects the realities of our society. This connection fosters authenticity and trust by creating a relatable and approachable persona among diverse stakeholders.
2. Entrepreneurial spirit: My journey as an entrepreneur taught me resilience and adaptability, and it showed me the value of innovation—lessons I have carried into my leadership at DIU. This action-oriented mindset encourages bold, goal-driven decision-making while inspiring others to think creatively and take ownership of their roles. Entrepreneurship is not just about taking risks but also about turning challenges into opportunities—a philosophy I strive to instill within the university's culture.

3 Passion for technology: Technology has always fascinated me as not only a tool but also a transformative force that can redefine education and society. My belief in leveraging technology for change has made DIU an early adopter of digital innovations in teaching, learning, and operational systems. This vision for a tech-integrated education ecosystem resonates across the university and positions us as forward-thinkers in an evolving global landscape.
4 Commitment to social responsibility: Leadership, in my view, must be grounded in ethical principles. My steadfast commitment to social responsibility drives me to uphold transparency, fairness, and accountability across all initiatives. These values not only guide decision-making at DIU but also foster trust and inclusivity within the community to encourage a sense of collective purpose among students, faculty, and staff.
5 Lifelong-learner mindset: Embracing the philosophy of lifelong learning has shaped my openness to the concept of change and the constant pursuit of improvement. I believe that adaptability and a willingness to learn are essential for thriving in today's rapidly evolving world. This mindset cascades across DIU, nurturing a culture of growth in which students and educators alike feel inspired to continuously seek knowledge and self-improvement.

Perception and Interactions

The interplay of these elements of my identity shapes how others perceive and engage with me as a leader:

- Approachable and empathetic: My rural roots and empathetic approach make me accessible to those I work with and instill trust and confidence in the leadership process.
- Visionary and forward-thinking: My emphasis on technology and innovation positions me as a leader who looks beyond the present to prepare for the future.
- Ethical and trustworthy: A commitment to fairness and social responsibility underscores my interactions, fostering respect and collaboration within the university and beyond.

Ultimately, these reflections on identity and perception affirm my belief that leadership is not merely about authority or ambition—it is also about building trust, fostering collective purpose, and empowering others to grow and succeed. This ethos continues to shape the legacy I strive to leave at DIU and in the broader education landscape.

Advice for Fellow Leaders

Based on my experiences leading Daffodil International University, I have realized that leadership in higher education is not merely about administration; rather, it is about vision and empathy and creating an environment in which everyone can thrive. With this perspective, I offer the following key advice to presidents, rectors, and chancellors who are seeking to leave a meaningful impact in the field of education:

1. Cultivate a vision with purpose.
    - Define a clear purpose: Leadership begins with clarity of purpose. What transformation do you want to inspire in your students, faculty, and community? What value does your institution bring to the world? A clear and well-defined mission is the foundation of success.
    - Inspire through communication: Vision is only effective when shared passionately. Engage your stakeholders—faculty, staff, students, and the wider community—with your purpose and inspire them to become part of a collective journey. A shared vision cultivates unity, trust, and motivation.
2. Empower your people to lead.
    - Trust and delegate: Positive leadership thrives on empowering others. Delegate tasks not out of necessity but with trust and belief in your team's ability. This encourages ownership, drives initiative, and cultivates a sense of belonging among your faculty and staff.
    - Mentor for growth: Leadership is also about nurturing leaders. Invest in professional development, mentorship, and upskilling programs. When you foster the growth of others, you strengthen the entire institution.
3. Harness the power of innovation.
    - Embrace technology: Technological advancement is redefining education, and it is critical to integrate cutting-edge technology

into every aspect of your institution. From virtual learning platforms to artificial intelligence–driven analytics, innovation must propel student success and institutional efficiency.
- Encourage creative solutions: Cultivate a culture in which creativity, experimentation, and risk-taking are celebrated. Progress happens when teams feel confident to challenge norms and explore new pathways.
- Adapt smartly: Change is inevitable. Work smartly and stay ahead of trends by being agile and adaptable. Institutions that evolve with societal needs remain relevant and impactful.

4 Foster a collaborative ecosystem.
- Build meaningful relationships: Collaboration across departments, disciplines, and external stakeholders is vital for institutional success. Build bridges that connect the university's mission with industry, government, and global community.
- Encourage open dialogues: Create an environment where everyone's voice matters. Transparency and open communication pave the way for trust and innovation by ensuring alignment and shared ownership of goals.

5 Champion student-centric leadership.
- Focus on holistic success: Higher education must go beyond academics. Nurture students' personal, professional, and ethical development to prepare them as resilient, adaptable leaders of tomorrow.
- Understand their needs: Actively listen to students' aspirations, challenges, and feedback. Your policies and decisions must reflect a deep understanding of their evolving needs in an ever-changing world.

6 Lead with empathy and integrity.
- Model positive leadership: Empathetic leadership drives loyalty, trust, and inspiration. Demonstrate compassion in your decisions, fairness in your policies, and accountability in your actions.
- Be transparent and accountable: Leadership is built on trust. Be transparent in decision-making and embrace accountability as a cornerstone of ethical governance.

7 Commit to lifelong learning.

- Stay curious: The world of higher education is constantly evolving. Engage with new ideas, learn from global trends, and stay informed about technological advancements and pedagogical innovations.
- Encourage continuous growth: Foster a culture where everyone—from students to faculty—sees learning as a lifelong endeavor. A leader's openness to learning inspires the same in others.

8 Engage with the community and world.

- Serve with purpose: Social responsibility is not an add-on—it is central to leadership in education. Actively engage with your local community and contribute to solving societal challenges. Education must be a force for good.
- Promote global perspectives: We live in an interconnected world. Encourage students to embrace global citizenship by fostering cross-cultural understanding, collaboration, and awareness. Prepare them not just as professionals but as changemakers in a global society.

Final Thoughts

Leadership is about service, not authority. It is about building a legacy through which the institution becomes a catalyst for transformative change—not just for students but rather for society as a whole. By embracing deep empathy, bold innovation, and steadfast commitment to purpose, higher education leaders can inspire growth, create opportunities, and empower a future in which learning knows no bounds.

Guidance for Aspiring Leaders in Higher Education

For those aspiring to lead as presidents, rectors, or chancellors, leadership in higher education demands preparation, adaptability, and commitment. Here is my concise yet impactful guidance, enriched with actionable insights:

1 Prepare for building a strong foundation.

- Deepen expertise: Establish academic credibility through advanced degrees, impactful research, and contributions to your discipline. Leaders with robust academic profiles are trusted and respected by their communities.

- Diversify experience: Venture beyond your specialization. Administrative roles, committee engagements, and cross-department collaborations provide the perspective needed to manage complex institutional ecosystems.
- Develop leadership skills: Prioritize mastering key skills like strategic decision-making, conflict resolution, and effective communication. Recent research shows that 70 percent of learning and development professionals believe that "mastering a broader range of leadership behaviors is essential for organizational success" (Harvard Business Impact 2025).
- Commit to lifelong learning: Stay updated on higher education trends, technological advancements, and global challenges. Institutions that evolve are often led by those who value continuous improvement.
- Network strategically: Leaders with expansive professional networks are one and a half times more likely to succeed. Seek mentors and connect with peers at conferences and workshops to learn from diverse experiences.

2 Embody the vision and purpose.

- Clarify the vision: Define the impact you want to make. A clear vision not only inspires but also aligns stakeholders to shared goals.
- Practice servant leadership: Prioritize the needs of students, faculty, and staff. A leader is most effective when they empower others to succeed.
- Embrace resilience and adaptability: Leadership is a journey of growth. Be prepared to navigate challenges with perseverance, viewing setbacks as opportunities to innovate.
- Demonstrate ethical leadership: Integrity and transparency are the cornerstones of trust. Leaders with a strong ethical compass foster enduring loyalty and respect.
- Exhibit passion for transformation: Let your passion for education fuel your actions. Higher education is a powerful tool for individual and societal transformation.

3 Embrace challenges as catalysts for growth.

- Step outside of comfort zones: Take on roles or projects that stretch your capabilities. Leaders who proactively embrace growth are better prepared to manage uncertainty.

- Learn from failures: Mistakes are part of leadership. Analyze them to refine your approach and foster resilience.
- Navigate change smartly: The higher education sector evolves rapidly—be agile. Institutions that thrive are led by adaptable leaders with data-driven foresight.

4 Build deep community connections.

- Engage authentically: Build meaningful relationships across your campus and beyond. Leaders who understand the pulse of their communities create more inclusive environments.
- Listen and empower: Data show that inclusive leaders who actively seek input from diverse perspectives are three and a half times more effective in achieving institutional goals.
- Serve society: Leadership extends beyond the campus. Embrace initiatives that uplift your local and global community to ensure that your institution contributes to the greater good.

5 Believe in your leadership potential.

- Convey confidence with purpose: Trust your abilities and let your passion guide you. Purpose-driven leaders inspire not just compliance but also commitment.
- Inspire others: Foster a ripple effect of positive change by letting your journey and dedication motivate others to pursue leadership.

Leadership in higher education is not about quick wins—it's a long-term commitment to excellence, innovation, and service. By strengthening your foundation, adopting the right mindset, and embracing challenges, you can leave a legacy that transforms individuals and societies for generations to come.

Championing Diversity and Advancement

At DIU, diversity is not just a goal—it's a driving force behind innovation, excellence, and societal impact. Our commitment to equity extends beyond policy, focusing on actionable initiatives that empower women and individuals from underrepresented groups. By fostering an environment that values inclusion, we are equipping our community to thrive in an increasingly interconnected and multicultural world. We have done so by:

1 Empowering women and driving gender parity.

- Ensure gender representation in leadership: Over the past five years, DIU has increased women's representation in leadership roles by 28 percent, with women now holding key positions in academic administration, research, and governance.
- Create mentorship programs: Through initiatives such as the Women's Leadership Network, women students and faculty are paired with accomplished mentors who guide their personal and professional growth. Research by Cornell University shows that structured mentorship programs for women increase promotion and retention rates by 15 to 38 percent (Conboy and Kelly 2016).
- Hold targeted leadership training: DIU offers specialized leadership workshops that focus on negotiation, strategic decision-making, and public speaking for women. These programs aim to bridge the confidence gap that often hinders women from pursuing top roles.

2 Supporting underrepresented groups to create equal opportunities for all.

- Uphold inclusive admissions: Our admissions policies ensure that 50 percent of scholarship opportunities are allocated to individuals from underrepresented groups, including those from remote areas, minority communities, and low-income families. This has led to a 40 percent increase in enrollment from underprivileged backgrounds over the past decade.
- Cultivate scholarships and financial aid: DIU has annually disbursed over $1.5 million in scholarships, enabling students who face financial constraints to access higher education and excel in their academic pursuits.
- Provide cultural awareness training: To promote sensitivity and inclusivity, DIU requires all faculty and staff to undergo regular training sessions on cultural awareness and unconscious bias, which creates a supportive campus environment for students from all walks of life.

3 Creating a safe and inclusive campus.

- Enact a zero-tolerance policy for discrimination: DIU has implemented robust systems for reporting and addressing harassment and discrimination. This includes anonymous reporting channels, grievance redressal committees, and immediate action protocols. Surveys indicate that 92 percent of students feel safe and supported on campus.

- Encourage diversity celebrations: From multicultural festivals to international student forums, DIU hosts more than twenty cultural events annually, showcasing the diverse backgrounds of our community and fostering a sense of belonging.
- Appoint diversity and inclusion ambassadors: Student-led ambassador programs ensure that inclusivity initiatives remain grassroots-driven, encouraging students to champion diversity among their peers.

4 Developing future leaders through inclusive leadership opportunities.

- Promote participation in governance: DIU ensures that women and individuals from underrepresented groups compose at least 30 percent of student government roles and club leadership positions, providing firsthand experience in decision-making.
- Mentor emerging leaders: Faculty-led initiatives focus on equipping aspiring leaders with the tools they need to overcome systemic barriers and take on influential roles in academia, industry, and beyond.
- Foster global leadership exposure: DIU connects students with international exchange programs and leadership summits to empower participants from diverse backgrounds in competing and collaborating on a global stage.

Impact and Progress

Taking these steps has led to:

- Increased leadership diversity: In the past three years, DIU has witnessed a 20 percent rise in women and individuals from minority groups who are occupying administrative and faculty leadership positions.
- Improved campus inclusion index: Feedback from our annual campus surveys highlights a 25 percent improvement in perceptions of

inclusivity, with students and staff reporting greater satisfaction with DIU's diversity efforts.

- Empowered alumni network: Many alumni from underrepresented groups have gone on to become influential leaders in their communities, demonstrating the ripple effect of DIU's commitment to equity.

Future Vision: Setting the Standard for Inclusive Education

DIU's ongoing mission is to lead by example in advancing diversity in higher education. By combining innovative policies, evidence-based practices, and a community-driven approach, we aim to create a university where everyone—regardless of gender, background, or circumstance—has the opportunity to realize their potential and contribute meaningfully to society.

Inclusion is not a checkbox; it is a journey. At DIU, we embrace this journey with unwavering resolve, knowing that by empowering individuals, we empower the world.

References

Conboy, Kaitlin, and Chris Kelly. 2016. "What Evidence Is There That Mentoring Works to Retain and Promote Employees, Especially Diverse Employees, Within a Single Company?" Cornell University School of Industrial and Labor Relations Student Works.hdl.handle.net/1813/74541.

Harvard Business Impact. 2025. "2024 Global Leadership Development Study." Insights. https://www.harvardbusiness.org/insight/2024-global-leadership-development-study.

4 Strategic Focus, Collective Strength

Fernando León García

President, CETYS University (Mexico)

Introducing My Institution

Nestled in the northwest corner of Mexico and neighboring California in what is referred to as the CaliBaja region, CETYS (Centro de Enseñanza Técnica y Superior) University is a private, not-for-profit institution. It was founded in

1961 by business leaders from the region with the mission of preparing well-rounded individuals to make significant contributions to the economic, social, and cultural development of Northwest Mexico and the US-Mexico border. CETYS has shaped leaders for more than six decades by creating synergies between academia, industry, society, and government. The CETYS University educational model is multi-experiential, humanistic, flexible, and global.

CETYS University currently has close to 8,200 students who are distributed across its three campuses (Mexicali, Tijuana, and Ensenada), and it offers over thirty-seven undergraduate and graduate programs as well as high school programs. Key learning outcomes embedded across the CETYS curriculum include entrepreneurship, social responsibility, internationalization, business and industry links, sustainability, and digital literacy. Roughly 85 percent of the student body are from within the state of Baja California, 11 percent from other states in Mexico, and 4 percent from California and other states in the US. CETYS is one of the top five private universities and one of the top twenty public or private universities in Mexico, and it is committed to delivering high-quality educational programs that support and impact regional development. Several key indicators that reflect the institution's positioning in Mexico are that 73 percent of its full-time professors have doctoral degrees (among the top twenty-five), 74 percent of its most recent graduating class gained international experience during their studies (among the top three), and the average employability rate of its graduates is approximately 95 percent per year(among the top ten). CETYS has close to 50,000 alumni and former students across different program levels.

With undergraduate and graduate programs organized around business administration, engineering, and social sciences and humanities, CETYS supports interaction with business, industry, government, and community through its three Centers of Excellence: Competitiveness and Entrepreneurship, Innovation and Design, and Human and Social Development. These centers have been instrumental in developing broad, deep, and substantive relationships with key industry clusters in Baja California, such as aerospace, electrical and electronic, automotive, medical devices, software development, and—more recently—semiconductors. More recent additions have been the Center for Viticultural Studies and the Institute for Sustainability Studies.

CETYS is one of only five universities in Mexico with institutional accreditation in the US and the only one to date that has full accreditation by the Western

Association of Schools and Colleges (WASC) Senior College and University Commission (WSCUC), one of about twelve across Latin America, and one of fifty around the world. CETYS is also among a handful of institutions in Mexico with program accreditation in the US (through the Accreditation Council for Business Schools and Programs (ACBSP) and ABET). In terms of the *Times Higher Education* Impact Rankings, CETYS has been ranked as 600–800 in the world in employability and economic growth as well as in gender equality. Regarding QS Stars, CETYS has achieved the maximum five-star rating in employability, academic development, environmental impact, and distance education and a four-star rating in internationalization. According to UI GreenMetric World University Rankings, CETYS is ranked 277th in the world in terms of sustainability, sixth among private universities, and twelfth among all participating universities from Mexico.

CETYS is strategically connected to higher education organizations including IAUP, the American Council on Education (ACE), the Council of Independent Colleges (CIC), the Hispanic Association of Colleges and Universities (HACU), the Council for Advancement and Support of Education (CASE), the Association of Governing Boards of Universities and Colleges (AGB), Association of International Education Administrators (AIEA), NAFSA: Association of International Educators, WSCUC, the Institute of International Education (IIE), the Association of American International Colleges and Universities (AAICU), AUAP, the International Association of Universities (IAU), the Federation of Mexican Private Higher Education Institutions (FIMPES), Asociación Nacional de Universidades e Instituciones de Educación Superior (ANUIES), Santander Universidades, the Consortium for North American Higher Education Collaboration (CONAHEC), and Consejo Latinoamericano de Escuelas de Administración (CLADEA).

Leadership Tenure and Defining Moments

I have been president of CETYS University since 2010, leading the institution on a major transformational effort called Vision CETYS 2020, focused on high quality, global competitiveness, learning communities, and sustainability. Based on a commitment to and tradition of strategic planning, the most recent effort involves Vision CETYS 2036, which intends to deliver transformative experiences; nurture a culture of innovation; create significant impact; and achieve national and international outreach, relevance, and recognition.

There have been several key moments that stand out during my 2010 to 2024 period.

First and foremost was the opportunity provided by the board and the outgoing CETYS president, Enrique Blancas de la Cruz, to meet during the second half of 2009 with more than fifty key trustees to inquire about their perspectives on the challenges and opportunities facing the institution. More than seventy academic and administrative leaders and faculty from CETYS were also in attendance. This provided a solid foundation upon which to begin the presidency at CETYS in January of 2010.

Second were two major events or challenges during the first quarter of 2010: inheriting a board of trustees with 100 members and experiencing a 7.2-magnitude earthquake in the region. The governance challenge was one that involved launching a deliberate, concerted, and planned effort with support from AGB that led to majorly revamping the structure and organization of the board of trustees. This was done under the tagline of "one dream, one team," with many milestones already achieved but still being worked on as a continuous improvement process. The earthquake shook the physical foundations upon which CETYS was offering and delivering programs (overwhelmingly face-to-face with an emerging use of technology) as well as planning its future development. The institution had to shift to distance and online learning mode quickly to provide the necessary continuity to students in their respective programs. There was not a single physical casualty, and all buildings were still standing but some required structural reinforcement. As a result of a strategic conversation with the board, a decision was made that an important component of the emerging CETYS 2020 development would include a redefinition of the campuses' buildings rather than just repair, and it therefore would involve more ambitious construction goals.

A third moment involved the culmination of a long, laborious, and carefully crafted process that led to US accreditation. CETYS was able to move from WASC candidacy in 2008 to initial accreditation in 2012. That was a crowning moment for CETYS, as it had first approached WASC in the 1990s and achieved initial eligibility in 2004. This provided a solid foundation to then pursue and be granted program accreditation by ACBSP and ABET. In 2017, WASC reaccredited CETYS through 2027. And in 2024, ACBSP reaccredited CETYS through 2034. WASC, ACBSP, and ABET were essential for CETYS to then engage in the *Times Higher Education* Impact Rankings and QS Stars.

A fourth moment involves the Covid-19 pandemic and post-Covid challenges and opportunities. The CETYS University community and the board of trustees all came together to rethink what the institution was doing, what needed to be adjusted to cope during Covid, and how to then reposition the institution for the post-Covid era. One important result of this has been the CETYS multi-experiential model.

Cutting across this fifteen-year period are the development and cohesion of a solid and empowered team that has allowed a shared sense of leadership in reviewing and embarking on the necessary changes to move from an institution known for its excellence in teaching to one that is now increasingly engaged in applied research and projects with business and industry, setting up the ambassadors or leaders or champions of initiatives such as internationalization, and positioning CETYS with global organizations including IAUP, ACE, NAFSA, CASE, AGB, HACU, AAICU, AUAP, WSCUC, IIE, AIEA, IAU, Santander Universidades, CONAHEC, and CLADEA.

Professional Journey

The early death of my father when I was in elementary school influenced my development. My father was Chinese and my mother Mexican, a product of the border dynamics between Calexico and Mexicali. Both of my parents believed in and supported the importance and far-reaching power of education; this mentality led to my attending elementary and middle school in the US (in Calexico), high school and undergraduate studies in Mexico (in Mexicali), and graduate studies that included an EdD at Stanford University. These cross-border, multicultural foundations and experiences have enabled me to navigate between contexts, acknowledging that being different does not necessarily mean that one is better than the other.

From middle school onward, I was extensively involved in activities outside the classroom, including but not limited to working to cover the costs of attending school, being a member of the basketball team, academic tutoring, and the student body council, and serving as a part-time teacher in high school mathematics, physics, and English. Accordingly, these experiences have influenced being able to be engaged in and draw from multiple contexts.

One life-changing experience involved working as teaching assistant to the then-president of CETYS, Dr. Félix Castillo Jiménez, who inquired about future plans. He encouraged me to pursue a doctoral degree so that I could return to CETYS to help the institution and the board chart out the continuing development and improvement of the university. Dr. Castillo's successor, Jesús Alfonso Marín Jiménez, also motivated and supported me so that I could pursue my doctoral degree at Stanford University.

My doctoral dissertation at Stanford University, under the guidance of Professors Lewis B. Mayhew and James G. March, focused on accreditation self-studies—a choice that proved to be pivotal for future activities at CETYS University and beyond, as the study provided exposure to leaders and contacts of key colleges and universities in the WASC region.

Another important experience for me has been taking part in the ACE Fellows Program. The exposure to key concepts, distinguished speakers, best practices, and numerous college and university presidents, in addition to my internship placement at The University of Arizona and California State University Monterey Bay, laid the foundation for what I have been able to pursue and accomplish during the past twenty-five years.

Serving under Dr. Jorge Klor de Alva as chief academic officer for the University of Phoenix/Apollo Education Group, I had a life-transforming experience from many perspectives. With the openness and support from my wife, Claudia, to move to Arizona and embark on what Dr. Klor de Alva described as an unleashing of all the potential that I had but didn't know with projects based in the US and involving potential partnerships in Europe, Asia, and Latin America. That was followed by my serving as chancellor of the City University of Seattle's International Division, leading the development and growth of CityU's programs, campuses, and sites outside the US, including Europe, Asia and Oceania, and the Americas. There I served as executive vice president for academic affairs and as co-acting president.

All of the above have been essential: returning to CETYS as the first alumnus president, strengthening the tradition of developing well-rounded individuals, achieving institutional accreditation (WASC) and program accreditation (ACBSP, ABET), employing high rates of doctorate-qualified faculty as well as excellent graduation and employability rates, and becoming the most internationalized university in Mexico. My extensive global engagement has led to several honorary doctorates from Vysoká Škola Finanční a Správní in

Prague, Czechia; Dimitrie Cantemir Christian University in Bucharest, Romania; Caucasus University in Tbilisi, Georgia; and NIMS University in Jaipur, India. In addition, I have been recognized among the top 300 leaders in Mexico (2019–24).

Distinct Contributions to Leadership

Being the first alumnus to become president of CETYS University with many diverse experiences over the years provided a broad, rich, and historically well-grounded perspective as I assumed the top leadership role at my alma mater. These experiences at CETYS involved interaction as a student; a part-time teacher in high school and later lecturer; athletic director; dean of students; director of planning and then, provisionally, director of institutional advancement; chief of staff; vice president for academic affairs; and, unofficially, chief international officer.

While I was technically away from CETYS University, I pursued my graduate studies at Stanford. For roughly a decade in leadership roles at US-based global institutions, I remained connected to the CETYS's board and to CETYS as an adviser or special consultant. Consequently, I was never really disconnected and always close enough to know about the main developments and challenges facing CETYS University.

This special connection, while at and out of CETYS University over the span of several decades, provided me with a unique angle to return and lead the institution: I had sufficient knowledge to be considered a local but enough distance from CETYS, coupled with exposure to the US and the rest of the world, to provide a global perspective.

Strategic connections and networking have been instrumental in raising the level of quality and profile of CETYS. It has grown from an excellent regional university among the best private universities in Mexico to become one of the top five private universities and the most internationalized institution in Mexico. Institutional improvement, transformation, and innovation at the institution have maintained, enhanced, and extended CETYS University's connections and been crucial to the profile that the institution has been able to develop over the past fifteen years. The following list includes some of these organizations, as well as the role I played on behalf of CETYS:

- IAUP: President 2021–24, chair of the IAUP Board 2024–27
- Asociación Mexicana de Universidades Privadas: President 2024–26
- WSCUC: WSCUC Commission, chair of the WSCUC International Accreditation Committee, chair of reaccreditation team for numerous WSCUC institutions
- ACE: Chair of the ACE Council of Fellows, chair of the ACE Commission on Internationalization and Global Engagement
- AGB: Member of the AGB Council of Presidents
- CASE: Member of the board of directors president of the CASE Latin American Regional Council
- CIC: Board member
- HACU: Member of the board of directors, chair of the Commission on International Education
- IAU: Member of the administrative board
- AIEA: Member of the Presidential Ambassadors Council
- NAFSA: Member of the board of directors
- AUAP: Member of the Advisory Council
- FIMPES: Member of Consejo de Directores, president of Comisión Permanente de Evaluación Actualización del Sistema de Acreditación, and president of Comisión Ejecutiva de Internacionalización
- ANUIES: Member of the Consejo Nacional
- Santander Universidades México: Member of the Consejo Nacional

Effective Leadership Strategies

There are several concepts that have been a part of my leadership experience at CETYS University.

In *Good to Great: Why Some Companies Make the Leap … and Others Don't*, author Jim Collins (2001) talks about having the right people on the bus. After an extensive round of meetings and conversations prior to the beginning of the presidency in 2010, it was clear that many of the leaders that were required for the next stage of development at CETYS University were already on the bus. What was needed, in many cases, was a possible repositioning and potential reenergizing opportunity. This meant having not only the right people on the bus but also the right people on the right seat on the bus. Accordingly, most of the teams that had been a key part of the development of the institution in the past were invited to continue in their roles, while others were offered alternative leadership roles. Overall, an overwhelming majority remained; as the years have gone by, some have since retired. There have been new additions, as required. It is perhaps among the faculty where the greatest change has occurred—less because faculty have left but more because the total number of full-time faculty has increased as enrollment has grown by more than 33 percent.

Unwavering commitment to both the mission and to quality programs has been essential in moving CETYS University forward to the next level. It has also been necessary to link its mission and programs to key performance indicators (KPIs) and to dashboards for periodic and systematic reviews.

Acknowledging and not being shy about starting and operating as an institution that is still an enrollment-driven institution allows all of the relevant parties to view student recruitment, admission, enrollment, and retention as essential, cross-functional elements that neither begin nor end with enrollment management.

Ensuring that leadership is viewed across the different levels and hierarchies of the university as empowering others to move forward on behalf of CETYS has been crucial. This includes promoting evangelizers and champions of strategic initiatives and priorities.

Reinforcing the need to have and recognize progress based on information and KPIs has further moved the institution to be driven more by data than by hunches, impressions, or opinions.

Making sure that there are mechanisms and processes through which there is recognition of commitment, progress, and achievement has been essential, whether it is a certificate, a token of appreciation, a special ceremony, a note from the office of the president, a bonus, or a promotion—anything possible that will convey to the university community that they are key and integral to the development and success of the institution.

Providing leadership development programs as well as faculty and staff development programs has been an important component to engage the necessary breadth and depth of talent that is required for the present and future of CETYS.

Establishing channels and conduits through which key areas of the institution come together for periodic and systematic communication and information sharing has worked wonders in terms of conveying that we are all part of one big effort to serve students. Keeping an eye on the annual budget and plans—but with an outlook on the long term and long-range goals—is also essential.

Personal Identity and Perception

Some colleagues have described my leadership at CETYS University as that of a president and a poster child. CETYS University has highlighted the fact that I am one of its graduates as well as an important part of the institution's development for many years. My identity as CETYS's first alumnus president figures prominently in student recruiting materials and diverse newsletters. My personal tie to the institution slides into conversation when I give interviews or field questions during presentations to CETYS faculty members, local town hall meetings, or regional and national events. In some ways, this puts a face to a success story about CETYS University.

As someone who relied on several scholarships and various jobs at the university to pay for college, I occasionally stress that working hard and seeking scholarships can be the path for others to move forward in life. Accordingly, raising and contributing money for scholarships and student experiences is something close to my heart. Roughly eight out of every ten students at CETYS receive some form of financial aid.

Given that I was also involved in athletics and extracurricular activities in the past, student development and success are an important component of my leadership agenda.

Having been on the sides of planning as well as institutional advancement, I am equally comfortable presenting the vision of CETYS to business, industry, and government leaders as I am to faculty or to potential donors. In a team effort with the board chair and several other key trustees, CETYS has been able to reach unprecedented levels of fundraising, including the establishment of the first endowed fund, the launch of the most aggressive construction effort in the history of CETYS, the securement of multiple donations of a million dollars each through multiyear pledges, and—more recently—the receipt of the largest single donation in the history of CETYS.

As previously expressed, my leadership espouses empowerment and the delegation of strategic roles; a belief in and reliance on the strength of my leadership team; a focus on strategic priorities rather than minutiae; the promotion of institutional evangelizers for key initiatives and as a reward for progress and achievement; a preference for KPIs and data-driven decisions that support the leadership development for those in core functions; an investment and belief in quality and quality improvement; and a belief in the synergy of CETYS across its three campuses rather than the strength of each campus on its own.

Advice for Fellow Leaders

- Know and show your commitment to the mission and quality of your institution. Link these to KPIs to dashboards for periodic and systematic reviews.
- As often as necessary, remind and reinforce across faculty and staff that the university exists to serve and support the development and success of students.
- Acknowledge the importance of enrollment as an institutional priority and a cross-functional task. To a great extent, financial sustainability is based on success in enrollment.
- Empower others to help move the institution forward.
- Promote evangelizers and champions of strategic initiatives and priorities.
- Reinforce the need to have and recognize progress based on information and KPIs and being data-driven rather than relying on hunches, impressions, and opinions.
- Ensure that mechanisms and processes are in place to recognize commitment, progress, and achievement at all levels, whether this is a certificate, a token of appreciation, a special ceremony, a note from the office of the president, a bonus, a promotion, a ceremony recognizing years of service, etc.—any and everything possible that will convey to the university community that they are key and integral to the development and success of the institution.
- Support leadership development programs as well as faculty and staff development programs, as these are all important components to ensure the necessary breadth and depth of talent that is required for the present and future of your institution.
- Establish appropriate communication channels and conduits through which key areas of the institution can periodically and systematically share information, thereby creating a sense of community.

- Establish a compelling and inspiring vision with appropriate engagement from the university community.
- Provide follow-up to the annual budget and plans but with an outlook on the long term and long-range goals.
- View and work with the board of trustees—and particularly the board chair—as a team.
- Have one or more colleagues, if possible, who can serve as a sounding board or mentors for best practices, ideas, challenges, and opportunities.

Guidance for Aspiring Leaders

If you have an aspiration or simple curiosity about whether leading an institution is in your nature and on the horizon for you, give yourself some time to learn about your strengths and weaknesses. Talk to sitting presidents about their experiences. While you can rely on the philosophy of CliftonStrengths—previously known as StrengthsFinder—to espouse and highlight your distinctiveness in a particular set of skills or experiences, a leadership position in higher education will likely require more than just your breadth of knowledge or reliance on your team's expertise. Spend some time trying to work on improvement of your weak areas.

A varied, broad perspective will provide you with better peripheral vision and understanding. Believe in yourself and avoid falling into the imposter syndrome trap. If you have the time and can secure the necessary resources, participate in a leadership development program.

Assuming you have the necessary rapport and trust with your leaders, talk with them about your future plans. Whether or not this leads to opportunities within or outside your current institution, it will put you on the path of personal and professional growth and fulfillment.

Nurture key relationships within and outside your institution. Networking is a very powerful and far-reaching tool for progression in higher education.

Share your plans with your family or your partner. Their support will be essential in what is commonly a very lonely path or experience, if it is not appropriately planned for or communicated.

If, in the end, you decide that the leadership of a college or university is not for you, you will have at least analyzed and clarified that your priorities and fulfillment are elsewhere. If your conclusion is that the leadership of a college or university is for you, make sure that you seek a reasonable institutional fit between the nature and context of the institution and your own profile.

Championing Diversity and Advancement

Although diversity in Mexico has been understood and promoted overwhelmingly from a gender perspective, it has only been recently that diversity in a broader sense is being promoted and addressed. In general, the prevailing notion had been that we are all Mexicans (rather than Mexicans with a distinction based in ethnicity, country, sexual orientation, or gender identity).

Accordingly, this section only reflects what has been done in terms of gender.

- Among the full-time faculty, 53 percent of the professoriate were women, with the Mexicali and Ensenada campuses above that percent and the Tijuana Campus below said percent.
- Out of four vice presidents, two were women and two were men.
- Regarding the campus deans, two were men and one was a woman.
- Concerning the deans of the systemwide colleges, two were women and two were men.
- With respect to campus-level directors of academic affairs, two were women and one was a man.
- In terms of the initiative on succession planning for the top twenty-five roles and functions at CETYS University, close to two-thirds were women.
- As part of said initiative, three out of six internal candidates for a future CETYS University presidency were women.
- Since 2019, six out of twelve CETYS participants in IAUP seminars on leadership development have been women.

Besides having a diversity, equity, and inclusion (DEI) statement for several years, in 2024 CETYS established the Equity and Inclusion Center, which is intended to raise the level of awareness about DEI, promote workshops on sensitivity toward and more active role regarding DEI across the institution, and act as a channel or conduit to address any issues or problems concerning DEI.

Reference

Collins, Jim. 2001. *Good to Great: Why Some Companies Make the Leap … And Others Don't*. Harper Business.

5 Strategic Focus, Resilience, and Global Impact

Ricardo Mairal Usón

Rector Magnificó, Universidad Nacional de Educación a Distancia (Spain)

Introducing My Institution

The Universidad Nacional de Educación a Distancia (UNED), over which I have the honor of presiding, was established in 1972 and is Spain's premier public institution dedicated to distance learning. Headquartered in Madrid, it operates sixty-one study centers across all Spanish autonomous communities and maintains a global presence with twenty-four centers in different countries throughout Europe, America, and Africa.

The mission of UNED is to provide accessible, flexible, and quality higher education to a diverse student body, regardless of geographical location or personal circumstances. By leveraging distance learning methodologies, UNED aims to promote lifelong learning and equal opportunities in higher education.

The unique attributes of our university could be summarized in the following points:

- Comprehensive academic offerings: UNED offers a wide range of programs, including thirty official undergraduate degrees, eighty master's degrees, and twenty-one doctoral programs. Fields of study encompass disciplines such as physics, chemistry, computer science, engineering, economics, philology, philosophy, history and geography, psychology, political science, law, and education.
- Flexible learning modalities: The university provides a blend of online and face-to-face sessions, accommodating students' varied needs. This hybrid approach allows learners to balance their studies with personal and professional commitments.
- Inclusive admission policies: UNED's open admission policy for undergraduate degrees, without grade cutoffs, enables a diverse range of students, including professionals and younger learners, to pursue higher education. Furthermore, we are the university that allows for 40 percent (approximately 8,000) of the students with disabilities in the whole Spanish system, as well as a great portion of the military and people in the correctional system. Regarding the latter, UNED has signed agreements with the former Ministry of Universities, the Ministry of Defense, and the General Secretariat of Penitentiary Institutions so that interns who are deprived of liberty in correctional institutions are not also deprived of the access to higher education.

Regarding the university priorities, the great challenge we are pursuing at the moment is ensuring financial support of our institution; namely, to secure an agreement with the Ministry of Science, Innovation, and Universities to obtain a long-term financial funding system (multiyear financial plan). Other than that, our current priorities focus on key goals such as internationalization, quality research, lifelong learning, technological advancement and inclusion.

As far as the international sphere is concerned, I am proud to say that we are the biggest campus in Europe and the only Spanish university that has twenty-four centers abroad, with an extensive capillarity that allows us to take our methodology and education "wherever you are," as our motto says. Also, and very importantly, as of December 2024, UNED is a key participant in OpenEU, the Open European. This partnership focuses on modernizing higher education with an emphasis on lifelong learning, inclusivity, and digitalization. The alliance addresses global challenges such as climate change, digital transformation, and democratic promotion.

In the technological arena, the university is committed to enhancing its digital infrastructure to improve the distance learning experience for all. This includes developing a common virtual campus and recognized microcredentials to facilitate continuous learning, upskilling, and employability.

We place a strong emphasis on quality research and on making higher education accessible to underrepresented groups, such as women in science, technology, engineering, and mathematics (STEM) fields; individuals with disabilities; residents of rural areas; and migrants. Efforts are therefore directed toward creating an inclusive learning environment that supports diverse student needs and success.

In particular—and considering the present complexity of the global situation—I am firmly convinced that we must foster knowledge and scientific rigor against any kind of dogmatism, hate speech, or misinformation, as these are so far away from the true values of academia. We undoubtedly must combat these negative issues but remain optimistic, and we must search for balance in all our movements and decisions.

All in all, through these initiatives, UNED continues to uphold its commitment to providing quality distance education and adapting to the evolving demands of the global educational landscape.

Leadership Tenure

I have served as president of UNED for more than six years, and I have had to face many defining moments. The most challenging by far has been the management of the university affairs and, in particular, the administration of final exams during the Covid-19 pandemic. This was an extremely tough situation in which we were obliged to provoke a change of paradigm. Our statutes state that final exams have to be carried out in situ at UNED premises, and therefore they are normally conducted in person by our faculty and students in all our physical centers in Spain and abroad. But on this occasion, we had fewer than three months to create a system of online exams for more than 150,000 students that would guarantee their quality and reliability. And I am proud to say that we succeeded in doing so, without any major complication being reported or experienced. However, I have to confess in all honesty that it was a very stressful situation that involved a great deal of previous work, effort, and sleepless nights for the government team and the entire UNED community. Once the lockdown was over, we returned to our policy of in-person exams; the online exam is now used on some occasions for practice on some subjects but never for final exams.

Professional Journey

My path to the role of rector of UNED has been deeply rooted in both personal commitment and professional milestones, as well as significantly shaped by previous roles and the challenges I faced during a pivotal period in Spain's economic history.

My previous tenure as vice-rector of research was instrumental in developing my leadership skills. During this period, I worked tirelessly to foster innovation and collaboration across our academic departments. Research is the cornerstone of any university's global contribution, and I prioritized creating opportunities for interdisciplinary projects, even in times of limited resources. This role also deepened my understanding of how knowledge production fuels societal progress, equipping me with the strategic vision required to guide our university through an era of rapid technological and educational transformation.

Subsequently, as vice-rector of academic staff, I was entrusted with the immense responsibility of managing one of UNED's most vital assets: its faculty. This position coincided with a period of financial austerity in Spain, which required difficult decisions and careful negotiation to ensure that academic quality was preserved despite budget constraints. I focused on supporting staff development, encouraging flexibility, and ensuring that morale and productivity remained strong under trying circumstances. This experience prepared me to make tough but empathic decisions that prioritize both institutional integrity and the well-being of our community.

These leadership roles were further complemented by my firm belief in the mission and impact of distance education. Through UNED, we provide access to quality education for students of all backgrounds, including those who might otherwise be excluded. My candidacy for rector was deeply informed by these values, as well as a vision for making education more inclusive, innovative, and globally competitive.

These experiences shaped me into a person who understands the inner workings of academic institutions as well as the challenges and opportunities that come with managing them during times of crisis. They gave me the resilience, strategic foresight, and empathy necessary to serve as rector and lead UNED into the future. My desire is that it will continue to thrive as a beacon of accessible, high-quality education.

Distinct Contributions to Leadership

First, I feel compelled to express my most profound recognition and respect for my predecessors, each of whom left an invaluable legacy that has shaped the institution into what it is today. As proof of this profound respect, one of the first events I organized as rector was a meeting with the ten professors that occupied the position of rector of UNED before me. Fortunately, at that time all of them were alive, and I had the honor and pleasure of being able to express my deep gratitude to them—because I firmly and honestly believe that gratitude has to be an inherent attribute in every leader. The efforts of my predecessor rectors have laid the groundwork for UNED's global recognition as a pioneer in distance education. Thus, my approach is not to replace their contributions but to build upon them by bringing a perspective that is logically shaped by my own professional experiences and the challenges of our current global landscape.

If I am to think about the defining features of my tenure, I believe I can assert that one of them is my commitment to fostering dialogue and conciliation. We are living in a time of profound social, political, and economic upheaval worldwide. These turbulent times, as I often refer to them, demand leaders who prioritize unity and collaboration over division. My leadership is centered on creating spaces for open dialogue among faculty, staff, students, and external partners because I believe that the best solutions come from collective intelligence. I see myself as a bridge builder who ensures that every voice in our university community is heard and respected, even amidst disagreement. I aim to lead with a balance of pragmatism and optimism to ensure that UNED survives and thrives in a rapidly evolving educational and technological landscape. My vision for UNED is one where education continues to be a unifying and transformative force.

Finally, my respect for my predecessors ensures that I approach this role with humility. I draw inspiration from their successes while striving to adapt to the unprecedented challenges of our time. In doing so, I aspire to leave a legacy of conciliation, innovation, and unity, ensuring that UNED remains a beacon of hope and opportunity for future generations.

Effective Leadership Strategies

At our university, as at many other institutions, successful leadership hinges on clear objectives, open dialogue, and measurable outcomes. As rector, I have adopted strategies that emphasize not only consensus-building but also accountability and critical self-assessment. This dual approach ensures that we maintain a collaborative spirit while also driving tangible progress toward our goals.

One of the most effective strategies I have implemented is the development and communication of a robust strategic plan for 2022 through 2026. This plan is a cornerstone of my leadership. It is built on two essential pillars:

1. Clarity and measurability: Unlike plans that remain vague or overly aspirational, the strategic plan sets out clearly defined objectives that are both qualitative and quantitative. These include specific goals for expanding access to education, enhancing digital infrastructure, improving student satisfaction rates, fostering internationalization, and increasing research output, among others. By making these objectives measurable, we ensure that progress is transparent and that success—or lack thereof—can be critically evaluated.
2. Continuous evaluation and reflection: To foster accountability, we have implemented mechanisms to assess our progress at regular intervals.

This allows us to identify areas where we excel and those where improvement is needed. Such critical reflection not only strengthens our strategic approach but also ensures that our leadership remains flexible and responsive to challenges as they arise.

Further, I have tried to integrate data-driven decision-making into the institution's leadership culture. Whether evaluating student performance, faculty productivity or operational efficiency, decisions are grounded in empirical evidence. This has been instrumental in ensuring that our actions are effective and aligned with our strategic goals.

Lastly, I have focused on fostering a culture of shared management. Successful leadership is not about acting unilaterally but about empowering others to take ownership of their roles in achieving institutional success. A good leader delegates authority but not responsibility; by delegating authority and providing the necessary resources, I have tried to cultivate a sense of collective commitment to our mission.

Personal Identity and Perception

As I have pointed out, my leadership style is deeply influenced by my belief in the power of dialogue, collaboration, and group work, as well as by the unique identity and global reach of our institution. My background, experiences, and values shape my approach to leadership, and I am fully aware that how others perceive and interact with me is directly tied to my ability to embody the mission and vision of UNED as both a national and international university.

First and foremost, my belief in the diversity of opinions is at the heart of my leadership philosophy. I am convinced that no single perspective or voice can capture the complexity of the challenges we face in higher education. For this reason, I approach leadership as a facilitator rather than a unilateral decision-maker, encouraging open dialogue and critical reflection. Whether shaping our strategic plan or addressing day-to-day challenges, I actively seek the input of diverse stakeholders—faculty, staff, students, and external partners—because, as I previously remarked, I know that the best solutions emerge from collective work and intelligence.

Second, my awareness of UNED's global presence, with sixty-one centers across Spain and twenty-four centers on three continents, profoundly influences how I lead and how I aspire to be perceived. I see UNED as a bridge between cultures and different knowledge fields, and I work to ensure that this identity is reflected in every decision we make. As a leader, I prioritize initiatives that strengthen our international partnerships; promote multilingual and multidisciplinary education as much as possible; and celebrate the diversity of our students, faculty, and staff. By embracing this global identity, I aim to reinforce the perception of UNED as not just a Spanish institution but rather as a leading example of multicultural and international education—especially now that we form part of the European alliance of open universities—OpenEU—which includes ten European universities as full members as well as four other universities as associated partners, four university associations, and eight nonacademic partners from different countries (industrial associations, digital networks, city and rural groups, and mentorship associations).

In this context, I am particularly mindful of how others perceive me in this role. I aspire to be seen not only as a steward of UNED's rich academic traditions but also as a forward-thinking leader who embraces innovation and collaboration. I strive for my leadership to be defined by openness, transparency, and humility—qualities that I believe help foster trust and mutual respect among the university community and our global partners.

In sum, my background and beliefs drive me to position UNED as a university that embodies unity through diversity. In an increasingly interconnected world, I see UNED as a model for how education can transcend barriers, borders, languages, and cultures. My goal is for others to perceive and interact with me as a leader who represents the shared values of our institution: inclusiveness, collaboration, and excellence on both the national and international stage.

Advice for Fellow Leaders

Based on my experiences as rector, my advice to other presidents, rectors, and chancellors is to approach their roles with a mindset rooted in humility, active listening, and a clear vision. Leadership in academia is not about dictating from the top but instead about guiding an institution through collaboration, showing respect for diverse perspectives, and having an unwavering commitment to the values of knowledge and science. Here are the key principles I would share:

1. Practice active listening and respect for all opinions: A successful leader understands that the strength of an institution lies in the collective wisdom of its community. Actively listening to faculty, staff, students, and stakeholders fosters trust and ensures that decisions are informed by diverse viewpoints. Even in moments of disagreement, respecting all opinions cultivates an environment of inclusivity and shared ownership, which is vital for institutional success.
2. Embrace humility and gratitude: As academics, we stand before the immense and ever-expanding fields of knowledge and science with humility. This perspective is essential for any scholar. Recognizing the limits of our own expertise allows us to value and be grateful for the contributions of others and reminds us that leadership is a collaborative journey. Humility also ensures that we remain open to learning and adaptable to the evolving needs of our institutions.
3. Foster respect and dialogue: Respect and dialogue are the cornerstones of academic leadership, especially in times of crisis or uncertainty. In moments of tension, it is the leader's responsibility to create spaces for constructive conversations to bridge divides and find common ground. The ability to engage in meaningful dialogue, even with those who hold differing views, is essential to maintaining unity and fostering progress.
4. Define a clear vision and path forward: Leadership requires clarity of purpose. As rector of my university, I have found that defining where I want to take the institution—and communicating this vision effectively—has been crucial. A clear and actionable plan provides a roadmap for the future, aligns efforts across the institution, and inspires confidence in the direction we are heading. This vision must be rooted in the institution's mission while also being adaptive to the changing global landscape.
5. Advocate for the values of science and knowledge: Above all, academic leaders must champion the values of science and knowledge as the foundation of progress and societal betterment. Upholding academic integrity, encouraging critical thinking, and fostering innovation are responsibilities that extend beyond the university to society at large. As

leaders, we must be advocates for education as a transformative force that addresses global challenges and promotes equity and opportunity.

My pithy advice to other academic leaders is to lead with humility and openness and to maintain steadfast commitment to the values of science and knowledge. By listening actively, fostering dialogue, respecting diverse opinions, and defining a clear vision for their institutions, they will surely be able to navigate the complexities of academic leadership and ensure that their universities thrive as centers of excellence and inclusion.

Guidance for Aspiring Leaders

To individuals aspiring to become presidents, rectors, or chancellors, my advice would center on preparing thoroughly, cultivating the right mindset, and prioritizing collaboration. Leadership in academia is a unique challenge that requires a combination of institutional knowledge, management experience, and inspirational leadership that unifies diverse teams. Based on my journey to becoming rector of UNED, here are the key recommendations I would share:

1. Develop a deep understanding of the institution and its governance: One of the most important steps in preparing for academic leadership is gaining comprehensive knowledge of the institution you aspire to lead. Understanding its mission, values, structure, and governance processes is essential. Familiarize yourself with how decisions are made, how resources are allocated, and how the institution interacts with external stakeholders. At UNED, where our governance spans national and international centers, having this knowledge has been indispensable in aligning leadership with the needs of the community and the broader context.
2. Build strong experience in management: Leadership requires more than academic credentials—it demands practical management experience. Seek roles that give you responsibility for budgets, personnel, and decision-making, as these will prepare you to handle the complex operational aspects of leading a large institution. In my case, my previous roles as vice-rector of research and vice-rector of academic staff helped me develop the strategic thinking and resource management

skills that are necessary to lead effectively. Look for opportunities to manage teams, projects, and resources, and try to learn and find the positive outcomes not only from successes but also from failures.

3 Prioritize teamwork and collaboration: Leadership is not a solo endeavor; it is a team effort. A successful leader surrounds themselves with talented, dedicated individuals and empowers them to contribute to the institution's goals. Recognize that the success of any project, whether strategic planning, research initiatives, or operational improvements, depends on group work and collaboration. Cultivate the ability to bring people together, foster mutual respect, and encourage shared ownership of decisions. Building a culture of teamwork and trust will be the foundation of your success.

4 Adopt a growth-oriented and resilient mindset: Leading an academic institution is both challenging and rewarding. To succeed, you must approach the role with a mindset that balances ambition and resilience. Be prepared to face difficult decisions, navigate moments of uncertainty, and manage competing priorities. At the same time, embrace challenges as opportunities for growth, both personally and for the institution. Maintain a focus on long-term goals and remain adaptable to change.

5 Engage with the broader academic and policy landscape: Aspiring leaders must also understand the broader trends that are affecting higher education—both nationally and internationally. Whether it is advancements in digital learning, shifts in funding models, or changes in societal needs, being informed about the external context allows you to position your institution for success. At UNED, our presence across three continents demands a global perspective, and I have found that staying engaged with international networks and policy discussions has been invaluable.

In summary, preparation for academic leadership requires a deep understanding of the institution, a background in practical management, and a collaborative mindset. Success comes from leading with honesty and integrity, building strong teams, and embracing challenges with resilience and a clear vision for the future. If you aspire to lead, approach the role with a sense of humility, a commitment to service, and an unwavering dedication to the mission of education and knowledge.

Championing Diversity and Advancement

At UNED, supporting women and individuals from underrepresented groups is a fundamental priority that is deeply embedded in our values and initiatives. We recognize that achieving equality and fostering diversity are not only moral imperatives but also essential to the advancement of knowledge and the enrichment of our academic community. To this end, we have implemented a range of policies, programs, and initiatives to actively promote gender equality and inclusiveness:

1 Our commitment to the equality plan: Our university has recently published its second equality plan, which outlines concrete measures to promote gender equality across all levels of the institution. This plan serves as a roadmap for eliminating glass ceilings and all barriers to equality, including actions related to recruitment, career advancement, and work-life balance. It reflects our unwavering commitment to building a university community in which everyone has the opportunity to succeed—regardless of their gender or background.

2 The Equality Office: Our Equality Office is at the heart of these efforts, working tirelessly to monitor progress, implement initiatives, and provide support to those who experience inequality. This office acts as a resource for faculty, staff, and students, ensuring that issues related to discrimination or gender bias are addressed effectively and that our policies promote a culture of inclusion and respect.

3 Education and research on equality: UNED's academic offerings include a master's degree in gender equality, which equips students with the theoretical and practical tools to address gender disparities in society. In addition to this, we organize numerous courses, workshops, and research activities on equality, encouraging academic inquiry and public discussion on this crucial topic. These efforts underscore our belief that education is one of the most powerful tools for driving societal change.

4 The Elisa Pérez Vera Award: One of our most prestigious initiatives is the Elisa Pérez Vera Award, named in honor of not only UNED's but also Spain's first woman rector. This annual award is a trailblazer in the pursuit of equality, recognizing outstanding academic work on gender equality and women's rights, and highlighting the critical contributions of scholars to this field. By celebrating and rewarding these efforts, we not only honor Elisa Pérez Vera's legacy but also inspire others to continue advancing equality through research and action.

5 Leadership by example: At UNED, we lead by example. More than 60 percent of the members of the university's government team are women, demonstrating our commitment to gender balance in leadership positions. This reflects our determination to create pathways for women to rise to the highest levels of responsibility and influence, breaking traditional barriers and reshaping the landscape of leadership in higher education.

6 Support for underrepresented groups: Beyond gender equality, UNED is committed to supporting individuals from all underrepresented groups. We actively work to ensure that our policies, academic programs, and research initiatives address the needs of marginalized communities. Our inclusive approach extends to fostering diversity among our students, faculty, and staff, recognizing that diverse perspectives are essential to academic excellence and innovation.

Through these efforts, UNED is proud to be at the forefront of promoting equality, inclusion, and diversity in higher education. We view this not only as a responsibility but as an opportunity to shape a more just and equitable society. By providing resources, education, recognition, and opportunities, we are actively empowering women and individuals from underrepresented groups to reach their full potential and to lead in their fields.

Conclusion

In conclusion, as rector of the Universidad Nacional de Educación a Distancia, I am deeply committed to fostering a leadership style that reflects the values of a collaborative spirit, an inclusive mindset, and a clear vision for the future. Drawing on my experiences and preparation, I have sought to create a culture of dialogue, respect, and critical reflection, ensuring that all voices within our diverse academic community are heard and valued. Through strategic planning, measurable goals, and data-driven decision-making, we continue to align our efforts with UNED's mission as a leader in accessible, multicultural, and multilingual education.

Our dedication to promoting equality and diversity is evident in initiatives such as the equality plan; the work of our Equality Office; our master's degree in gender equality; and the prestigious Elisa Pérez Vera Award, which honors exceptional contributions to gender studies. With women composing over 60 percent of our government, we demonstrate that leadership in academia must be representative and inclusive.

To those aspiring to academic leadership, I emphasize the importance of humility and respect, active listening, and understanding one's institution. Leadership is a collective endeavor rooted in teamwork and collaboration. It is only through the shared commitment of our university community that we can uphold the values of science, knowledge, and equality, positioning UNED as a beacon of excellence on both the national and international stage.

6 Leading Through Data and Diversity

Gonzalo Mendieta

Rector, Universidad de Las Américas (Ecuador)

Introducing My Institution

The Universidad de las Américas (UDLA) stands as a leading private higher education institution in Ecuador. Founded in 1995, UDLA has rapidly evolved into the country's largest private university and is distinguished by an innovative educational model focused on comprehensive student development.

What began as a focused academic portfolio in business administration, communication, and technology has expanded to include diverse fields such as medicine and health science, engineering, law, culinary arts, architecture, and music. Today, UDLA operates several campus locations in Quito that feature state-of-the-art infrastructure and specialized laboratories. Our main campus, UDLAPark, spans over 65,000 square meters with EDGE Advanced certification for sustainability. Additional campuses include Granados, Colón (specializing in dental health sciences), and Nono (our experimental farm with forty-six hectares dedicated to agricultural sciences, veterinary medicine, and sustainability research).

The university's mission centers on "forming competent and entrepreneurial professionals with an international-global vision, committed to society and based on ethical principles and values." Our core values include academic freedom, pursuit of excellence, innovation, humanism, respect, integrity, resilience, inclusion, and environmental respect.

In 2019, UDLA achieved a significant milestone by becoming the first Ecuadorian university to receive international accreditation from the Western Association of Schools and Colleges (WASC) Senior College and University Commission (WSCUC). Currently, we hold the most international accreditations among private universities in Ecuador, including ABET for engineering programs, Consejo Mexicano para la Acreditación de la Educación Médica (COMAEM) for medicine, and Comisión Nacional de Acreditación (CNA) and Accreditation Council for Business Schools and Programs (ACBSP) for business programs.

Our academic community comprises over 20,000 students who are supported by more than 1,600 professors. UDLA has graduated over 36,000 professionals, with impressive employment outcomes.

The university maintains a strong commitment to research, ranking among Ecuador's top three universities in scientific production. Through innovative initiatives in education, research, international partnerships, and sustainability, UDLA continues to advance its position as a leading institution of higher learning.

Leadership Tenure

I have served as rector of UDLA since 2019, following six years as academic vice rector. My journey in higher education leadership spans over three decades, including roles as dean of academic affairs at Universidad San Francisco de Quito; director of institutional effectiveness; and deanships across disciplines including medicine, technology, and hospitality.

The defining moments of my tenure have revolved around three key achievements: international accreditation, research advancement, and institutional resilience.

The most significant milestone was successfully leading UDLA through the WSCUC accreditation process, making us the first Ecuadorian university to receive this international recognition. Another defining achievement has been the remarkable growth in research productivity, with UDLA rising to become one of Ecuador's top three universities in scientific production. This transformation from a primarily teaching-focused institution to one that balances teaching with impactful research represents a fundamental shift in our identity.

Additionally, successfully navigating the institution through the global pandemic demonstrated our resilience. By implementing innovative approaches to educational delivery while maintaining financial sustainability, we ensured continuity and quality during unprecedented challenges.

My leadership approach emphasizes using data-driven methodologies that reflect my background as a statistician while building collaborative relationships with stakeholders. I currently serve as a representative for private universities to Ecuador's Higher Education Council, the president of the Confederation of Private Universities and Schools of Ecuador, and a board member of the International Association of University Presidents.

Professional Journey

My path to university leadership has been characterized by a willingness to accept diverse challenges, which allows me to develop a comprehensive understanding of higher education from multiple perspectives. Rather than following a conventional linear trajectory, my career has involved both vertical advancement and strategic horizontal moves across different academic and administrative domains.

One of the most formative experiences was serving as the interim dean of the School of Culinary Arts, a position distant from my statistical expertise. During this tenure, I led a curriculum transformation by integrating theory and practice through the establishment of a professional restaurant and bakery where students applied their learning under academic supervision. This innovative model proved so successful that other universities across Ecuador have since replicated it.

Similarly, serving as interim dean of the College of Medicine expanded my understanding of diverse academic ecosystems. These experiences outside my discipline showed how an external perspective can overcome entrenched barriers to innovation. Coming from outside the disciplinary tradition allowed me to question assumptions and introduce new approaches when faced with a common obstacle: "This is how we've always done it."

After completing my doctoral degree in the United States, I began my academic career at a public university in the US. This international experience provided a valuable perspective on different models of higher education. Beyond academia, my experience as chief executive officer of a market research company enhanced my understanding of organizational management and data-driven decision-making in practical contexts.

The culmination of these experiences led to my appointment as rector of UDLA in 2019. My path illustrates that there is no single route to university presidency; rather, it is the breadth of experiences and willingness to embrace challenges that best prepares one for the multifaceted demands of institutional leadership.

Distinct Contributions to Leadership

UDLA has been led by only three presidents throughout its history, with each leadership transition marking a distinct phase in the university's development. Until 2007, UDLA was a small, private institution with programs primarily in law, business, and design. The leadership transition that year initiated rapid expansion, with many new programs added and the student population growing fivefold.

When I joined as academic vice rector in 2013, I brought a distinctively different focus to leadership. Rather than continuing to emphasize growth alone, I concentrated on strengthening the university's academic reputation—a fundamental shift from expansion to consolidation and quality enhancement.

My distinctive approach has been characterized by three key elements. First, I initiated an aggressive hiring campaign for full-time faculty with advanced degrees and research credentials. This shift from a primarily adjunct model to one with dedicated full-time academics created a stronger foundation for academic excellence. Second, I developed a comprehensive research initiative that transformed UDLA's identity. My leadership approach emphasized that research excellence and teaching quality should be complementary priorities rather than competing ones, which resulted in UDLA's recognition as one of Ecuador's leading research institutions. Third, I brought a strong commitment to international standards through accreditation.

Perhaps most distinctively, my leadership philosophy has balanced ambition with sustainability. While maintaining the growth trajectory, I've focused on financial sustainability to pursue academic quality and institutional resilience—an approach that proved invaluable during the pandemic when many rapidly expanded institutions faced difficulties.

Through these contributions, UDLA was transformed from a growth-oriented teaching institution to a comprehensive university with significant research output and international recognition.

Effective Leadership Strategies

Throughout my career, I've developed strategies that have proven effective in fostering institutional success and innovation. Central to this philosophy is a collaborative approach that empowers colleagues to take ownership of their ideas and responsibilities.

I consistently find that allowing colleagues to come forward with their own initiatives yields remarkable results. Viewing those under my leadership primarily as peers rather than subordinates encourages them to take both initiative and responsibility for their teams and projects. This distributed leadership creates a more agile, responsive organization.

This philosophy proved particularly effective during our institutional accreditation process. By trusting team members with significant autonomy, we developed a comprehensive self-assessment that led to success. Similarly, empowering research leaders to organize themselves was key to developing an efficient and sustainable research model.

I recognize this approach occasionally has failures. When initiatives don't succeed, I maintain awareness that ultimate responsibility remains with me. This balance between delegating authority and accepting accountability creates an environment where innovation can flourish without fear of failure.

My leadership philosophy was shaped by a football coach who used to say, "We have a plan for the game, now it's your turn to play." His wisdom that "the wins are ours; the losses are mine, and as for the draws—who knows" has guided how I distribute credit and responsibility. By celebrating collective successes while shouldering the burden of setbacks, I've fostered a culture of experimentation and continuous improvement. Having worked under leaders who trusted me with new ideas, I'm committed to creating similar opportunities for those I now lead.

Personal Identity and Perception

My upbringing has fundamentally shaped my leadership style. I was raised to embrace the possibility of failure—it was always better to try and fail than not to try at all—while understanding that failure should never result from insufficient effort. This duality continues to influence my approach to leadership.

As rector, I encourage my team to explore different approaches without fear of failure; I emphasize that while success has merits, failure often presents the greatest learning opportunities. This perspective has fostered an institutional culture that values innovation and calculated risk-taking, essential for transformation.

My fascination with mathematics and science led me to pursue degrees in statistics, establishing a foundation for decision-making rooted in critical thinking and evidence. This analytical background—uncommon among university presidents, who typically come from fields such as law, business, or humanities—offers a distinctive lens for examining institutional challenges that is particularly valuable in today's data-rich environment.

In a recent conversation with fellow university executives, we reflected that none of us had planned administrative careers when completing our doctoral studies. Yet we found ourselves in leadership positions because we were willing to step outside our comfort zones at critical junctures—reinforcing a core value from my upbringing: leading by example.

This combination of analytical thinking and personal authenticity shapes how others perceive my leadership. Former colleagues often characterize my style as firm but gentle, suggesting that I've balanced high expectations with empathy and support. My international academic experience has given me a global outlook, positioning me as a bridge between Ecuadorian higher education traditions and global educational practices.

Advice for Fellow Leaders

While each institutional context presents unique challenges, my tenure in Ecuador has taught me valuable lessons that may resonate with fellow university leaders.

As both a former provost and now as a rector, I've navigated profound changes in Ecuador's higher education landscape, including constant regulatory shifts and challenges to private institutions. Success in such circumstances comes through patience and open communication—especially with those who hold different perspectives. No gap may be bridged without establishing and maintaining communication channels.

The fragmentation of traditional orders globally brings new complexities to higher education. Some even suggest the possibility of extinction for traditional universities, while the emergence of artificial intelligence adds further uncertainty.

Amidst these challenges, university leaders must remember our fundamental purpose as knowledge creators and educators. Education has become less and less about knowledge transmission and ever more about creating environments for students to develop durable skills and become lifelong learners who are capable of adapting to whatever future awaits.

This vision requires several leadership approaches. First, maintain focus on your institution's mission and values. External pressures may push toward short-term reactions, but mission-aligned decisions prove more sustainable.

If we hold fast to our mission, we'll find a way forward even in challenging circumstances.

Second, cultivate strategic patience. Higher education transformation occurs over years, not months. Maintaining consistent direction while adapting tactics to changing conditions is essential for institutional stability.

Third, build robust communication networks within and beyond your institution. In uncertain times, transparent communication and regular engagement with all stakeholders become critical.

Finally, invest in developing the next generation of academic leaders. Creating pathways for talented faculty and administrators ensures institutional sustainability and brings fresh perspectives to ongoing challenges.

Guidance for Aspiring Leaders

For those aspiring to university leadership, I offer advice based on both successes and missteps throughout my career. The path to university presidency is rarely linear—few of us envisioned this trajectory when beginning our academic careers.

First, develop a strong foundation in your discipline. Excellence in scholarship and teaching creates credibility and provides analytical frameworks that will serve you well in leadership.

Second, seek opportunities to lead at various levels within your institution. Whether chairing committees, directing programs, or serving as a department chair, these experiences provide crucial insights into university operations. Each role I've held has provided unique perspectives that inform me in my work as rector.

Third, cultivate institutional thinking rather than departmental. Leadership requires expanding your perspective to consider how decisions affect the entire university ecosystem as well as understanding interconnections between academic affairs, student life, finance, and external relations.

Fourth, develop comfort with calculated risk-taking. Leadership often requires making decisions with incomplete information and balancing innovation with institutional stability.

Fifth, build your emotional intelligence. Technical competence alone is insufficient; the ability to understand perspectives, manage conflict constructively, and inspire collaborative action is fundamental to university leadership.

Sixth, commit to continuous learning about higher education beyond your institution. Engage with national and international organizations to understand broader contexts and distinguish between institution-specific challenges and sector-wide trends.

Finally, remember that presidency is not an achievement but a position of service to an institution's mission Effective leaders find fulfillment in advancing the institution's impact on education, research, and society.

Championing Diversity and Advancement

Two extraordinary women have significantly influenced my understanding of gender equality and approach to inclusive leadership. The first is my mother, whose teenage ambition to become an engineer was thwarted in Ecuador of the early 1950s, when engineering was virtually closed to women. She became a high school mathematics teacher in all-girls public schools, sharing at our dinner table stories of prejudices she encountered when encouraging women students to pursue higher education, particularly in science, technology, engineering, and mathematics (STEM) fields. Her dedication extended beyond the classroom—she often visited families of promising students to persuade reluctant parents to support their daughters' academic aspirations. Through these experiences, I learned that addressing inequality requires not just awareness but also concrete action.

The second influential figure is my wife, who was among the few women to study mathematics at our university and became the only woman in her cohort by the end of the first year. Sharing courses with her, I witnessed the differential treatment she received from predominantly male faculty. Her determination earned respect, and she graduated as the first woman mathematician in Ecuador, later becoming the first woman dean of engineering and first woman provost at her institution.

These examples have fueled my commitment to promoting diversity and advancement in all positions that I have held from the classroom to the rectorate. At UDLA, this materialized when I became academic vice rector through an extensive faculty hiring plan with dual goals: recruiting the highest quality academics while achieving gender parity. What initially seemed challenging proved straightforward with unbiased selection processes. Today, UDLA has been recognized by *Times Higher Education* as the top university in Ecuador for gender equality.

My advocacy extends beyond UDLA through participation in national and international higher education organizations, advocating for systematic changes to make academia more accessible and equitable. University leaders have a special responsibility to model the inclusive excellence we hope to see more broadly in society.

7 Transforming Through Strategic Renewal

Juan Camilo Montoya Bozzi

Rector, Universidad Autónoma de Bucaramanga (Colombia)

Introducing My Institution

The Universidad Autónoma de Bucaramanga (UNAB), located in the city of Bucaramanga, Colombia, is a private nonprofit institution recognized for its academic excellence, innovation, and commitment to regional and national development. It was founded in 1952—initially as a primary and secondary education school that was based on the principles of freedom, autonomy, and democracy—a time when Colombia did not offer educational alternatives that were autonomous and independent from the state or the Catholic Church. That school, Instituto Caldas, grew over time; in 1969 the institution began offering higher education undergraduate programs, starting with business administration and later adding law, public accounting, and social communication.

Today, we can affirm that we are an organization that provides high-quality educational services at all levels, from the preschool level at Instituto Caldas all the way through doctoral programs offered by UNAB. In total, we offer 107 higher education programs approved by the Colombian government, and UNAB has held Institutional Accreditation of High Quality since 2012 and is currently valid until 2029.

Our programs serve nearly 9,000 students in higher education with about 775 professors. Since 1952, Instituto Caldas has grown consistently; today, it serves around 1,000 students and is recognized in our region for its quality and affordability.

In recent years, especially after the pandemic, we undertook an important strategic process that allowed us to build a clear value proposition, make significant adjustments to our organizational structure, and develop clarity and discipline, based on the objectives and key results (OKRs) methodology outlined in *Measure What Matters: How Google, Bono, and the Gates Foundation Rock the World with OKRs* by John Doerr (2018).

Our five values are:

1 Institutional philosophy

2 Educational highways

3 Knowledge-generation for regional development with a global vision

4 Access alternatives

5 Unique higher education experiences

After this process, we firmly believe that effective action around these values—with tangible benefits for our students and other stakeholders—will make UNAB a relevant and distinctive institution with a long-term vocation of positive influence in Colombia.

Our current priorities, related to the aforementioned attributes, are focused on areas such as:

1 Expansion, modernization, and transformation of our academic programs portfolio, striving for greater flexibility for students in terms of emphases (minors), educational modalities, and possibilities for articulation across different levels of education.
2 Offering various financing and access alternatives for our students through short- and medium-term loans, income contingent loans, and scholarships enabled by our philanthropy efforts and new institutional advancement capabilities.
3 Strengthening academic and research capabilities of our professors through various instruments, aiming to focus research projects on the social, economic, competitive, environmental, and political development priorities of northeastern Colombia.
4 Modernizing our physical and technological infrastructure across all campuses through plans that allow us to prioritize new projects and better utilize our current infrastructure.
5 Diversifying income by developing alternative investments in businesses related to higher education, seeking to strengthen our long-term financial sustainability. Likewise, operational growth in primary and secondary education is also of interest to our institution.

Leadership Tenure

I took office in December 2018, after serving on the board of directors for six years. My professional background was not in academia but rather in executive leadership roles within business associations including Asociación Nacional de Empresarios de Colombia (ANDI) and the Bucaramanga Chamber of Commerce, as well as with companies in industries such as construction, mining, and private equity.

My selection as UNAB's rector by the board aimed to drive a generational transition at the university, following the board of directors and the General Assembly of the United Nations approval of corporate governance measures that encouraged the retirement of individuals already receiving pensions and adopted other ethical standards to prevent conflicts of interest. Moreover, at that time there was a need for leadership more strongly focused on the university's competitive strategy and ensuring financial sustainability after the completion of a national government demand-subsidy program, Ser Pilo Paga. Through this program, UNAB enrolled about 35 percent more students than the average between 2014 and 2018. The growth in revenue generated by that program overshadowed the need to strengthen various capabilities and the need for tighter control over the institution's overall spending.

The year 2019 was challenging due to the start of the generational transition in senior leadership positions and the budget deficit we had to tackle beginning in February, resulting from a poor outcome in undergraduate enrollment. In general, the university had grown accustomed to rising demand, which also led to higher spending and an inertia that was not sustainable in this new context.

That fiscal year closed with a deficit that was not as large as it might have been, thanks to austerity measures we managed to adopt in collaboration with the new administrative and financial vice rector, who had experience in higher education and was selected for the job in July 2019 with the help of a search firm.

In 2020, we began with a significant focus on austerity, basing our annual budget on a stricter approach. The undergraduate enrollment campaign fared better than anticipated, thanks to increased involvement from all the deans and program directors. The entire team had to contribute to this effort, not just the promotion and marketing group.

And of course, as it happened worldwide, everything changed in March 2020 with the onset of the Covid-19 pandemic. After a few intense weeks that resulted in a successful transition to remote teaching and learning, the university's financial situation called us to make decisions to reduce personnel expenses in both academic and administrative areas. We did so with the support of the board of directors and the direct involvement of the deans and heads of administrative departments.

Looking back, I believe that my previous executive experience was crucial at that time for recognizing the need to act immediately and send a clear signal to the entire institution regarding the necessity of operating efficiently and initiating a strategy and transformation process—especially given the university's low cash reserves at that point and the end of public programs supporting demand.

The pandemic, coupled with the gradual return to normal operations during 2021, ultimately strengthened the university's finances, allowing us to begin processes of strategic reflection and action, as well as investments in physical and technological infrastructure. In order to bolster our financial position, create cash reserves for growth projects, and be better prepared for future tough times, we created an endowment with very clear guidelines and an executive committee of experts to oversee its resources responsibly.

This positive story of strengthening was nonetheless marked by the pain of losing several members of UNAB's academic and leadership team, including the chairman of the board of directors, with whom I had a close personal and professional relationship.

In addition to being painful for everyone, that moment was significant as it did not create a disruption in the university governance. The board of directors unanimously appointed as chairman the member who was serving as vice chair, and we were able to continue in a spirit of unity to protect and strengthen the institution for the long term.

Professional Journey

My academic background in business at the undergraduate level (Universidad de los Andes) and graduate level (American University, from which I earned a master of business administration), along with my professional track record in business associations and as chief executive officer of notable regional companies, afforded me a broad perspective on the region, the country, and the world.

An enterprise-focused vision of organizations in general, a clear understanding of the importance of comprehending markets to compete successfully, and my strong interest in regional business development and competitiveness have, in my opinion, been extremely valuable in my role as rector.

My experience as executive president of the Bucaramanga Chamber of Commerce, regional manager of ANDI, and chief executive officer of prominent companies in the region gave me the opportunity to understand regional challenges related to competitiveness, human talent development, and improving local government.

Additionally, in nearly all of my previous leadership positions, I stepped into those roles after they were held for many years by another executive. In that sense, the challenge of initiating a transformation at UNAB and leading a team that needed renewal and alignment with a new strategy was not unfamiliar to me, even though the university's leadership environment itself was new.

At UNAB, I found a board of directors that was deeply committed to the institution, had no internal power struggles, and offered full support for a leadership approach that was bound to be challenging and whose results would take some time to materialize.

My previous experience has also been very helpful in building a diverse network of contacts that are now useful in my role as rector.

Finally, the experiences I had leading corporate and competitive strategy processes in those business associations and private companies prepared me to propose the strategic and transformative process we are now undertaking at UNAB.

I am convinced that UNAB needed a shift toward a far more concrete and rigorous strategic process that would clarify for the team the choices to make. Our goal is to remain relevant in the markets in which we compete, without compromising the university's nature, its founding principles, or its active commitment to freedom, autonomy, and democracy.

Distinct Contributions to Leadership

So far, my primary focus has been to lead a transformation process for the entire organization, grounded in understanding the capabilities built over recent decades, and developing greater clarity and strategic discipline at both the corporate and competitive levels. Guided by that strategy—seeking to define our differential attributes within a value proposition—we have realigned the organizational structure in critical processes, driven generational renewal, modernized the program portfolio, and launched a capacity-building process for research, creation, and innovation. In summary, I have been in constant pursuit of consistency in decision-making and the development of stronger leadership and management skills among the entire leadership team.

At the same time, we have strengthened the university's finances by improving our promotion and marketing capabilities, controlling expenses, and prioritizing infrastructure investments based on our infrastructure plan. Our financial control measures allowed us to build a healthy cash position and create an endowment to accumulate reserves, enabling the university to make bigger investments and address unexpected risks.

My focus has been on preparing the organization to better respond to the needs of the regional environment and to establish the capabilities that will allow UNAB to endure sustainably over the long term.

We are a relatively young university that started offering higher education programs in 1969. My predecessors (two rectors over the previous forty years) focused on growing undergraduate and graduate programs, building campuses, and developing the fundamental academic capacities of a regional university primarily dedicated to undergraduate and graduate professional education.

Between 1995 and 2005, the institution solidified these efforts through its first national quality accreditations for undergraduate programs and later achieved institutional accreditation in 2012. In 1997, the School of Health was founded and substantially increased the university's size. Significant innovations were also introduced with technical and technological programs and new modalities such as online and dual, the latter based on the German model. These innovative approaches, at the time they were introduced, have greatly influenced our current strategy, which aims for an increasingly flexible program portfolio that integrates multiple levels of education and modalities.

My leadership style has also been based on fostering greater closeness and ongoing communication with our stakeholders. I like open and direct conversations to understand the challenges faced by students, faculty, and staff at UNAB. I also frequently communicate with the entire community about progress, achievements, and challenges we face as an institution. Although being accessible and having open communication with all our stakeholders should not be surprising in a positive leadership approach, in our case it does represent a contrast with previous rectors whose leadership styles were more traditional and hierarchical.

Effective Leadership Strategies

After six years as rector, and after several conversations with members of my team, I can summarize the main areas of management and leadership I have pursued with the following five points.

- Leadership based on ongoing conversation and approachability, aiming to build shared purposes that guide our reflection, execution, and accountability
- Empowerment of a team that is empathetic, resilient, and supportive, which faced and overcame the pandemic amid painful human losses, thanks to innovation and the effective use of educational and technological capacities already in place within the organization
- Internal strategic clarity, focused on the external environment and the market, enabling us gradually to become a more modern university with a strong organizational culture, a vocation for lasting impact, and the ability to adapt to global educational trends
- A vocation for regional and national service aimed at generating the greatest positive impact; to this end, we have developed deeper relationships with the surrounding community—fostering regional competitiveness, social innovation, and culture through increased research and outreach activities financed with external resources
- Financial strengthening achieved through managing for sustainable growth and a shared responsibility in the efficient use of resources, seeking to reinvest as much as possible to bolster our human talent, modernize and expand infrastructure (both physical and technological), and save for future challenges and long-term goals

In many aspects of the strategic process and management, we have relied on the objectives and key results (OKRs) methodology. This approach has allowed us to articulate our aspirations and goals while also defining the specific intermediate actions that will help us achieve them. Its implementation has been a constant learning process and, at times, challenging for many academic leaders who were not familiar with management and tracking tools. Day-to-day operations supported by OKRs and the definition of the university's value proposition have helped many academic leaders develop stronger leadership and management skills.

Additionally, as I mentioned earlier, listening to the community through various forums—such as Un Café con Juan Camilo—has created closer connections and the possibility of open, constructive dialogue between the rector and the university's diverse stakeholders.

Personal Identity and Perception

In particular, I would highlight the deep connection between my paternal family and the region, as well as with UNAB, and my professional background, which has combined leading business organizations that promote regional development and competitiveness—always rooted in a professional yet close, straightforward, and open relationship with every collaborator.

Regarding the first aspect, I believe my identity includes a special family trait of strong ties, hard work, and interest in the economic and social development of my region (the state of Santander and the city of Bucaramanga). For decades, my parents and my paternal family have demonstrated this regional commitment through their work in business, public service, civic, and trade association activities. With respect to UNAB, which is governed by a broad and diverse group of regional citizens and leaders, my paternal family has maintained a close relationship with the university's growth and governance from its founding until its more recent history—first through my grandfather, who was part of the founder group, and later through an uncle who served as rector for twenty years in two separate terms.

As for the second aspect, my knowledge of the local context allows me to have a broad perspective on social and economic development, enabling me to see how UNAB can become more than a traditional university and gradually evolve into a more powerful and influential development agent in areas of interest to the community that fit with our academic capabilities.

In this regard—and given that I do not have a background as a professor or researcher—I strive to remain open and respectful on academic matters, which are led by the provost, the deans, and our faculty. The combination of a broad perspective on regional development; the need for a modern, focused, and sustainable university; and the high-quality academic and research vision allows us to maintain an open and balanced dialogue that I believe benefits the institution's long-term future.

As for how my leadership is perceived, I believe people appreciate my friendly, unassuming, and executive style of seeking solutions and acting swiftly when facing the various challenges we encounter on a daily basis.

Advice for Fellow Leaders

My main tips and recommendations are as follows.

Care for and strengthen the working relationship with the board of directors through transparent interactions, focusing on agreeing upon the institution's overarching vision and transformative initiatives. In that regard, it is essential to avoid scenarios of co-management or board interference in day-to-day matters, which fall under the responsibility of the rector and the executive team.

Devote substantial effort to building strategic clarity and helping teams pinpoint their priority actions and maintain execution discipline. In this strategic process, I believe it is essential for the institution's leaders and collaborators to be the main architects of the strategy rather than relying too heavily on sophisticated, and often costly, consultants. A strategy built and championed by the team itself—though it may appear basic or less sophisticated—often has a higher likelihood of being executed successfully within the expected time frame.

While working on strategy, it is equally important to understand the organization's critical cultural traits and lead a process to define the desired culture. Every organization has certain behaviors that need to be discontinued and others that should be adopted. Clear cultural traits shared by most team members will be key to enable successful performance.

Together with enhanced strategic clarity and a shared vision of the desired organizational culture, it is also important to involve the entire team in the details of annual budgeting in order to have them on board with the purpose of sustainable growth in financial terms. The more rigorous the rector and vice rectors are in setting budget goals and limits, the greater the responsibility and empowerment for the team to use resources in ways that best serve the strategy. This message is especially important in private, nonprofit universities that must be profitable in order to reinvest and compete in an increasingly challenging and uncertain market.

Finally, permanent and close communication with key stakeholder groups is crucial to maintaining open dialogue, sensing the concerns and sentiments of the community, and addressing both small and major needs in a timely manner—needs that, without such channels, the rector might never learn about. Additionally, this proximity shows all collaborators that the rector stands with them and is available to talk openly about university affairs and their well-being.

Guidance for Aspiring Leaders

Get to know the institution's identity. Dedicate time to talking with people who are familiar with the university's history—its origins, challenging moments, governance style, and the main leaders within the university community, among other aspects.

Develop a mental framework for leading the university's strategy, aiming for clarity on distinctive traits, big and ambitious goals, and fundamental transformative projects that require the rector's constant attention.

Be aware of the pace of changes and be mindful that—even though universities need change and the environment is evolving rapidly—not everything can or should be changed in the short term. True, high-impact transformations happen through steady progress with the involvement of key collaborators and leaders across the university.

Cultivate time management. Adopt a structured approach to effectively manage your time, striving to balance the demands from external and internal parties who want the rector's attention (macro, micro, internal, external, social events, etc.) with moments for focused thought and reflection. Additionally, protecting personal and family time is critical. Rectors must develop and maintain routines for exercise, reading, recreation, and good habits that enable a healthy family life and the energy to be effective in leading the university.

Championing Diversity and Advancement

At UNAB, which is an institution grounded in liberal principles and autonomy, we have taken on the responsibility of adopting policies and protocols that promote equal treatment for all members of our community.

Regarding women in leadership positions at UNAB, I can affirm that they have always participated in roles such as deans, provost, and leaders of various departments and programs. On a personal level, I have always felt very comfortable working with women and place great trust in their judgment and capacity to lead teams and carry out projects rigorously and transparently.

Additionally, concerning the handling of discriminatory situations and violence against women and diverse groups, we approved in 2022 our policy for the prevention and response to gender-based harassment and violence. This measure was crucial for forming a gender committee, which has led to the implementation of the protocol that enables us to address cases of gender-based harassment and violence that may occur at UNAB. The committee has been very proactive in receiving reports and undertaking corresponding investigations, which have in some cases involved employment decisions regarding university officials.

We will continue to expand collective awareness of respecting the rights of all members of our university community and take the necessary actions to apply our regulations.

Reference

Doerr, John. 2018. *Measure What Matters: How Google, Bono, and the Gates Foundation Rock the World with OKRs*. Portfolio.

8 Building Communities, Driving Success

Tomás D. Morales

President, California State University, San Bernardino
(United States)

Introducing My Institution

California State University, San Bernardino (CSUSB) is a preeminent center of intellectual and cultural activity in inland Southern California. The San Bernardino Campus (SBC) opened in 1965; the Palm Desert Campus (PDC) opened in 1986, with a permanent site granted in 1994. The university serves approximately 18,000 students each year on its two campuses, and it graduates approximately 5,000 students annually. CSUSB is one of twenty-three universities that compose the public California State University (CSU) system.

CSUSB is an anchor institution in San Bernardino and Riverside counties. Together, these counties geographically make up one of the largest bi-county regions in the United States. Comprising 27,000 square miles and serving close to five million residents, Southern California's Inland Empire is larger than ten US states. San Bernardino County itself is the largest county in the Lower 48. CSUSB is the only member of the CSU system with campuses in both these counties. The region has one of the lowest baccalaureate and graduate degree attainment rates in the nation—and one of CSUSB's goals is to increase these graduation rates.

CSUSB continues to climb in national rankings, both overall and in specific disciplines. For example, it has climbed in the national rankings for social mobility (*The Wall Street Journal* has CSUSB as third in the US for 2025), has been designated as a Research 2 university by the Carnegie Classification of Institutions of Higher Education (raising its status from a regional university to that of a national university), and has earned the Equity Champion of Higher Education Award in 2021, 2022, and 2023 by The Campaign for College Opportunity for its efforts to serve transfer students.

The vast majority of CSUSB students are the first in their families to attend college or university. Additionally, CSUSB has been a designated Hispanic-Serving Institution since 1994 and a designated Minority-Serving Institution since 2009. In November 2023, CSUSB was recognized by the American Association of State Colleges and Universities (AASCU) with the AASCU Excellence & Innovation Award for Diversity, Equity, and Inclusion Leadership. The university has also earned the prestigious Seal of *Excelencia* certification for 2024–27 from *Excelencia* in Education for demonstrating through data, evidence-based practices, and leadership the ways in which it is intentionally serving Latino students.

CSUSB's five academic colleges offer more than seventy undergraduate degrees, master's degree programs, and a doctoral program, as well as certificates. The four goals of its current strategic plan comprise student success; faculty and staff success; diversity, equity and inclusion; and internationalization.

With CSUSB's goal of student success—which informs everything at the university—the campus seeks not only to increase the college-going rate in the Inland Empire but also increase the college completion rate. It is necessary to have students arrive on campus as college ready as possible to help them persist in their college careers. Students also need to see college-going as accessible, particularly if they come from families without a history of attending college.

CSUSB utilizes several tools and methods to achieve these goals. For example, it is vital to establish partnerships with organizations and initiatives that promote the importance and the accessibility of college-going within underrepresented communities. Onboarding and CSUSB's Summer Bridge Programs also help students to prepare to transition to undergraduate life during the summer before their first term begins.

Once students are enrolled and have begun their course work, as either first-year or a transfer students, other supports are offered to encourage persistence and, eventually, graduation. They include intrusive advising and financial accessibility to a college education (this is a particular need in the US), as well as encouragement of student participation in clubs and organizations, education abroad, athletics, theater and music productions and performances, research opportunities with faculty members, and community engagement. Finally, the university recognizes and celebrates the diversity of its student, faculty, and staff populations, ensuring that CSUSB is an inclusive space—that is, all are welcome here, and no one is to be excluded or bullied because of differences.

What is foundational to CSUSB's efforts across the board is seeing that all university decisions and actions are data-based. For example, creating a strategic plan intended for actual use means the university has also designed an implementation plan to accompany it. Then, at the end of each year, the campus assesses what it has done.

Effectiveness cannot remain theoretical: it needs to be tested and continuously improved based on data.

Leadership Tenure

I was selected as the fourth president of CSUSB in May 2012. Since that time, I am proud to have overseen the following achievements, which I firmly believe have made our university stronger, more student-centered and have created a sustainable path for the future. From 2012 to 2025, some of the highlights have been that CSUSB has:

- Created the President's Cabinet and worked together to build a data-based leadership model, which has evolved and spread throughout all areas of the university
- Committed to student success, which has led to various innovative summer bridges and other student and academic support services
- Completed CSUSB's first major fundraising campaign and successfully raised $54 million while doubling the university endowment; currently exceeded the $200 million goal of our second campaign
- Developed the institution's unique Diversity, Equity, and Inclusion (DEI) Board as a reflection of CSUSB's existing pride in its diversity and in recognition of the need for building DEI into the structure of all university operations—an ongoing goal of mine
- Recognized that the best way to support and help lead the success of the region has been achieved through partnerships focusing on education; for example, the university spearheaded the first truly bi-county initiative to improve college attainment, resulting in the founding of Growing Inland Achievement, a 501(c)(3) nonprofit organization
- Applied a comprehensive, all-inclusive, and organically directed planning model to create and implement:
  - Two all-campus strategic plans
  - A campus master plan for each of the university's two campuses
  - A rethinking of the campus's DEI efforts
  - A conversion of the university from the quarter system to the semester system
  - Two CSUSB all-university reaccreditations
- Conceived and completed (or are in the process of completing) the following facilities construction:
  - A new building for the College of Extended and Global Education
  - An extension to the student union
  - A new dining commons and student housing
  - A building in the process of being repurposed to accommodate a new master of science in physician assistant (MSPA) program, an initiative to address the urgent need for trained medical professionals in our region

    - A forthcoming 500-seat performing arts center (scheduled to open in spring 2025), which will serve both our campus community and the larger community
    - A forthcoming student services building at CSUSB PDC
- Addressed climate change by:
    - Securing Leadership in Energy and Environmental Design (LEED)–certified status for our new buildings
    - Continuing sustainable energy and green processes
- Navigated successfully the shutdown related to the Covid-19 pandemic, which meant that the university:
    - Expanded the means of delivering instruction
    - Created a Wi-Fi access program when the campus was closed
    - Created a laptop lending program for those without access to these devices in their homes
    - Pivoted practically overnight from onsite to remote education and then managed the transition back to in-person instruction and services
- Instituted new programs and initiatives during my tenure by:
    - Developing the MSPA program (mentioned previously), to be implemented in 2025
    - Growing the cybersecurity program and options
    - Establishing the Randall W. Lewis School of Entrepreneurship and Innovation
    - Launching a course materials savings program for students
    - Joining the State of California's College Corps program, which offers internships for students to provide them with funding, transferable experience and career connections
    - Signing initiatives such as a data-sharing memorandum of understanding that allows CSUSB to help more students gain access to CalFresh, a food program particularly important for students with food insecurity

Building partnerships has also been a key goal. They have included relationships with our local K–12 public schools; the local, municipal, and state governments; the local business community; local civic organizations; as well as our regional community colleges and fellow regional universities. The aim has been to build a robust and sustainable cradle-to-career pipeline, as education is truly the conduit to improve individual lives and the lives of families and communities.

Professional Journey

Prior to assuming the CSUSB presidency, I served as president of the College of Staten Island of the City University of New York; in various capacities at California State Polytechnic University, Pomona, including as provost and vice president for academic affairs, vice president for student affairs and professor of education; and as vice president for student affairs and dean of students at the City College of New York.

In my over forty-nine years of working in higher education, I am one of the few higher education administrators in the United States who has held senior administrative positions at the three largest public university systems in the nation: The California State University, the State University of New York, and the City University of New York.

I am a proud product of US public education, from elementary school through doctoral degree. I have also spent my career at US public universities within the three public university systems I mentioned.

Equally important to my own educational journey and work history is the fact that I am a first-generation college student who gained admission through the Educational Opportunity Program (EOP). This is an initiative that both opens doors and supports students who might have never believed they could attend college. I have had this in common with so many of the students who matriculate at the universities where I have worked and held leadership positions.

I am grateful to all my mentors who provided me with the advice and encouragement to keep me moving forward in meeting my academic and career goals.

I am also incredibly proud to share that my own mother resumed her education after her youngest son went off to college. She completed her GED certificate or high school equivalency credential and then earned an associate degree, baccalaureate degree, and a master's degree in social work. She spent much of her professional career serving families in the New York City's South Bronx neighborhood, one of the poorest congressional districts in the US. Hers is an example I keep close to my heart and which continues to inspire me.

I have therefore committed my higher education career to giving back by serving as a champion for student success, on whichever campus I found myself serving.

I truly believe in the students I have worked hard to support over the years as they have made their way toward a degree. I believe today in CSUSB's students here in the Inland Empire—I see their potential. And I continue to see that the way forward to their achieving this potential is through access to higher education. But I also know that higher education in our region cannot do it alone. Rather, it is through the partnerships we build that will secure a cradle-to-career pipeline to transform lives and the communities of San Bernardino and Riverside counties.

Distinct Contributions to Leadership

The first four presidents of CSUSB have all been very different individuals. My immediate predecessor was also a first-generation college student and a product of the public schools of New York City for his K–12 education. However, I am the first Latino president of CSUSB. That fact, along with my EOP background, means I have a great deal in common with many of our students. I have been where many of them have been. I therefore hope I can demonstrate to them that higher education is one of the best ways I know to build a pathway to a fulfilling, successful career and life and that the door is also open for them—a higher education degree is possible.

Ultimately, however, I am the president for all the students at CSUSB. It means initiatives such as DEI are intrinsic to—they truly cannot be removed from—my focus on student success. And it is why student success has been a throughline to my approach as an educator and administrator in higher education from the start of my career.

In my view, the answer to enhancing the promise of economic mobility across the US is education. Education is how we better the lives of those who enroll as our students. This is how CSUSB can have an appreciable economic impact on our region as well as the lives and families of these students.

My experience and background make me aware of and sensitive to the lived experiences of first-generation students or any students who are forging a path for themselves, their families, and their communities.

Effective Leadership Strategies

Over the years, I have learned that effective leadership requires trust. And further, people need to have confidence in one another to work together productively. The foundation of that trust is ethics. Administrators, faculty, and staff also serve as role models and mentors. Leading with ethics sends a message to students on how they should act and behave while they are students and then after graduation.

While the cliché is true that as president the buck stops with me, major campus initiatives need to involve the whole campus as discussions are held and recommendations made. The organic, all-university approach to major initiatives at CSUSB has resulted in two practical and implementable strategic plans; a master plan for each campus; two reaccreditations; a campus transition from a quarter to a semester system; and a thorough review of the university's DEI practices to ensure that these principles are structurally and systemically embedded across all university operations, from classrooms to building maintenance.

I have hired individuals for my cabinet whom I believe to be outstanding in their respective areas. This means I respect their expertise. I should not need to do their job for them, even though I am ultimately the person responsible for decisions made during my presidential tenure. The way forward is by building a team that both understands your perspectives and vision, as president or chancellor, while offering a diverse set of ideas as feedback to clarify and strengthen the ultimate decisions that I must make as the university's leader.

Another foundational item for me in leadership is the role of data. I believe we must utilize data as the source of decision-making. CSUSB follows a path of continuous improvement, which includes examining the metrics and qualitative feedback from initiatives and adjusting them so that what is provided—for one example, in terms of recruitment and support throughout a student's academic journey—continues to be aligned with student needs.

It is important to ensure that the makeup of the student body, faculty, staff and administrators reflects the composition of the community where the institution is embedded (if it is a diverse one). And, if that local community is not very diverse, a healthy and diverse campus population should be consciously built through recruitment and hiring. It also means including access to international opportunities and exposure, both on campus and through study abroad or faculty exchanges. I truly believe that students have the richest educational experiences through exposure to individuals and cultures that are different from those in which they were raised.

Finally, keep student success at the heart of all you do as a university president. Know what the best high-impact practices are and then work to bring them to your campus initiatives and programs. That will help guide you throughout your presidency.

Personal Identity and Perception

My personal identity, first and foremost, comes from my parents and my siblings. They taught me that moving ahead and making a difference in bettering our own lives would take hard work and persistence. I began taking on part-time jobs when I was still in school, and that persistence and focus has helped to build my career.

I drive myself hard, and I expect the same of those who work with and for me—we have a responsibility to our students and to our university to do the best we possibly can do and succeed as much as we possibly can. When we make errors, actual lives are impacted. So, I know I can come across as demanding to my staff and my cabinet. However, they can also see that these are the same demands I am making on myself.

Advice for Fellow Leaders

To my fellow leaders: I greatly respect your success and hard work that has brought you to your leadership position. Therefore, any advice I give is likely redundant or, to be honest, is shaped by the conditions of managing a mid-sized public university in the US in the twenty-first century.

Nevertheless, my advice includes:

- Ensure that you build a strong leadership team. Build partnerships with your local, regional, and larger state or district community. When everyone tries to go it on their own, you end up with a lot of people all repeating themselves and reinventing the wheel. That is not necessary with a partnership. You share what you have learned, and you build on that knowledge; it allows you to move forward more quickly and effectively and, I would argue, on a sounder footing.

- Ensure that the decisions you make are data-based. Remember that it starts and ends with the students. How do you build student success? What are high impact practices that have been proven effective with students in your own countries?
- Ensure that students take ownership of their own educational journey. The university can provide support, but the will and motivation need to come from each student's own commitment.
- Ensure that students are thoroughly ready to begin their college career on day one and, if not, identify their deficits and how they should be addressed.

Guidance for Aspiring Leaders

If becoming a university president or chancellor one day is your goal, I would strongly advise you to reach out. Build connections. Build a community. And look for the helpers. There are always people out there who are available to mentor you, but sometimes you need to be the one to ask. Don't be afraid to ask for help—put out your hand and introduce yourself. (I also recognize that this is a very American perspective and approach; other cultures may have different best practices.)

Join professional organizations in your field. As you advance in administrative positions, learn what the top professional organizations are and get involved with them. Run for their boards. Build a network. That way, you increase the number of people who know who you are; they may support you with letters of recommendation or nominations for future positions.

Take the opportunity to gain additional leadership training through programs. For example, in the US, both Stanford University and Harvard University have special leadership programs, as do organizations such as the American Association of State Colleges and Universities (AASCU), which has the Millennium Leadership Initiative.

It is also important to know that serving as a university president or chancellor can be very isolating and lonely. You will always need colleagues, so be generous with your collegiality. Reach out to your counterparts at nearby institutions when they are hired or promoted or depart for other opportunities. These friends and colleagues will protect your confidence, will be honest with you, and will be there to support you without judgment.

Don't be afraid to build partnerships where possible. Build relationships and programs with your local and regional K–12 schools, two-year institutions, fellow universities, local and regional governments, state or district governments, the business community, civic leaders, and leaders of nonprofit organizations. To build economic success, you need education. And, to build an effective cradle-to-career pipeline, it takes all sectors of the community to come together, share data, and keep each entity from wasting time and resources if they are reinventing the wheel by sharing best practices.

At CSUSB, we view ourselves as an anchor institution here in inland Southern California. Students come from the region where we are located, and this is the region we are dedicated to supporting. To build students' success—the number one aim at CSUSB—means we need to partner with local organizations and consortia to help build that success. This means that we must transmit to students and faculty the region's needs and the ways in which they may serve, but we must also let the institutional partners and the general public know who the students are and the rich resources they bring to the Inland Empire's future.

Championing Diversity and Advancement

I firmly believe that a more diverse institution is a stronger institution. I realize I am speaking from the perspective of a US citizen in the twenty-first century, a nation which is on track for achieving a level of racial, ethnic and gender diversity that the eighteenth-century drafters of the US Constitution could not even have imagined. And it does, naturally, cause fear and backlash—change is always difficult. But I truly believe this is the best path forward for US higher education and the country.

I have supported aspiring women leaders in the university to attend women-focused higher education leadership workshops or participate in the HERS (Higher Education Resource Services) Leadership Institute, for example. I supported the creation of an annual women's leadership event at CSUSB SBC; it has continued to grow and develop since its inception and to bring new leaders to the fore with each new cycle and cohort.

DEI is always foremost in my mind in the area of hiring. Not, as some continue to argue, by employing someone above their skillset because they check a particular box on gender, ethnicity, or race, but rather by asking if we have identified all the potential candidates for the search. How do we hire the top candidates in whom our diverse student body might also see themselves? I have created the positions of co-chief diversity officers; among their other responsibilities, they provide training and oversight on both the staff- and the faculty-hiring sides.

A male-only cabinet or campus leadership would send a message to women students, faculty, and staff that there is a ceiling they cannot breach. If I look around and see that my cabinet is becoming all men, I know that I am not doing my job as a twenty-first century academic leader.

I have supported projects such as CSUSB's Project Impact Program in the James R. Watson & Judy Rodriguez Watson College of Education. This initiative encourages men from underrepresented populations to go into public K–12 classrooms to assist young men of color, so they do not drop out of school and that they continue to attend and complete college. There is a growing gender divide in higher education in the United States, and that is even greater with students from underrepresented populations. Having living examples interacting with them while they are still in school sends an important message to these young men that education has value and is an accessible pathway to their futures.

Here at CSUSB, all of our students are valued—regardless of where they were originally born or where their parents were originally born. We believe that access to education should be valued and treated as a right guaranteed to all, as education is the best way forward to building a better life for oneself, one's family, and one's community. We need to hold onto the truth, in this moment, that we are all fellow human beings and therefore deserving of the human and civil rights that should be afforded to all.

Our DEI efforts can be most effective if we have access to reliable and current data about those studying, teaching, and supporting our educational mission. With that foundational understanding in mind, for example, CSUSB partnered this past year with the University of California, Los Angeles's Higher Education Research Institute (HERI) to gather strategic plan baseline and climate data for staff and faculty. HERI conducted this survey during the 2023–24 academic year (AY). Staff and faculty participated in separate surveys with different sets of questions tailored to each group. This survey will be repeated as part of our strategic plan for years three (AY 2025–26) and five (AY 2027–28). In the meantime, results have been provided to CSBSU's Office of Institutional Research for staff and faculty.

This all goes to say, DEI is not a phrase or string of words that I parrot to check off a box. It is intrinsic to who I am as an educator and an educational leader. I remain committed to it as I continue serving as president of California State University, San Bernardino.

9 Leading with Perseverance and Conviction

Letlhokwa Mpedi

Vice-Chancellor and Principal, University of Johannesburg (South Africa)

Introducing My Institution

In 2005, then–Minister of Education Professor Kader Asmal established the University of Johannesburg (UJ) as a single higher education institution that would provide both technikon and university programs through the merger of the Rand Afrikaans University (RAU), Technikon Witwatersrand, and the East Rand and Soweto campuses of Vista University. This merger was more than just a structural change; it was a bold step toward bridging educational divides and ensuring that quality tertiary education was accessible to all.

The commitment of these three founding institutions laid the groundwork for a university that not only fosters excellence but also contributes meaningfully to addressing pressing societal challenges. We began as the new kids on the block as we forged a new identity steeped in transformation. In the decade following the merger, we built an identity around our collective expectations and Pan-Africanism. The next period produced a university aligned with global excellence and stature as we carved a meaningful space for ourselves in the Fourth Industrial Revolution (4IR) and began to imagine what a truly African university represented. We have built on that legacy now with a commitment to societal impact and sustainability. Last year, we launched our new strategic plan to take us to 2035.

If we consider sustainable approaches to be a resounding clarion call for our generation and the generations to come, then we are tasked with the responsibility to respond accordingly. Though often considered through a narrow lens, universities have an expanded role. We must lead in addressing ethical, moral, political, and social questions. I call this societal impact: the tangible effects of our research and work in the broader world.

This shift takes us beyond academic boundaries to engage directly with economic, social, and cultural spheres. Our purpose is not only to share knowledge but to inspire individuals to make meaningful contributions to society. UJ has long embraced the need to innovate boldly while grounding our actions in core values that promote continuity, inclusivity, and humanity.

We understand that alongside our commitment to academic excellence, we have a responsibility to ensure our approaches reflect purposeful progress. We have a duty to equip others not only with knowledge and skills but also with a commitment to ethical leadership and social responsibility. The core theme and outcome of this strategy is societal impact and sustainability to ensure that all UJ activities—including research, teaching, learning, and collaboration—contribute to bettering society and promoting sustainability.

Our mandate is simple: UJ provides a holistic, world-class education that goes beyond formal instruction to prepare students as resilient, critical thinkers who make a positive societal impact. We aspire to lead international research from an African and global south perspective.

Our research—driven by values of impact, innovation, inclusivity, and integrity—utilizes advanced technologies to promote sustainable living in a digital age. Our values guide transparent communication and accountability while our organizational agility enables us to collaborate effectively with communities, supporting a sustainable future and positive societal change.

Leadership Tenure

I became the vice-chancellor and principal of UJ in March 2023. The launch of our new strategic plan has been an incredible highlight. Its development was an intensive and iterative process that included contributions and feedback from various corners of the university.

What has emerged is a document of which I am really proud. In fact, *Higher Education Transformation in Africa: A Quest for Epistemological Rupture*, a volume edited by Emnet Tadesse Woldegiorgis, Logan Govender, and Dennis Zami Atibuni, includes a chapter on senior managers at UJ both past and present. It outlines how strong leadership at UJ has balanced efficiency with social justice and thus expanded access while advancing knowledge production.

Clear communication and branding have secured institutional buy-in and embedded our focus, while rigorous assessment ensures strategic alignment across all levels; a collaborative, solutions-driven culture reinforces these efforts. This structured approach has enabled UJ to thrive in a competitive higher education landscape and is the strong basis on which we have established our new strategy.

Professional Journey

Throughout my childhood, my father encouraged me to be a lawyer and my mother instilled a strong sense of discipline in me and sparked my love for education. For many years, I wanted to be the best criminal lawyer in the country until I began to develop a fascination with academia and the power education wields. Like many of our students at UJ, I am a first-generation graduate.

It is my very beginnings at Vista University and later at RAU that have led me here. My passion for labor law and social security formed within those very walls. At the Max Planck Institute for Foreign and International Social Law, I began to understand the value of approaching education through the gaze of societal impact. And so it was the encouragement of my parents, the advent of opportunities that I never considered to even be a possibility, and a passion for academia and the law that informed my journey.

Distinct Contributions to Leadership

There must be a focus on doing good. Importantly, this was built on the legacy of my predecessors and this is an important point to make. Here, I must make note of Professor Tshilidzi Marwala's focus on our shifting context and goal for UJ to emerge as dynamic and active participants in the 4IR. This is a legacy that took root in Professor Ihron Rensburg's commitment to transformation, equity, access, and Pan-Africanism. It is in their perspectives that the idea of societal impact emerged. We now need to ensure that we continue on this trajectory with greater attention paid to sustainability and development.

We have made some strides in these areas already—the goal, however, is to ensure that our future-centric stance stresses the importance of humans and their needs. This is the very idea our new strategic plan is rooted in.

Effective Leadership Strategies

First, understanding that universities do not operate in isolation has been an important strategy. It has been valuable for me to stay informed about global trends in education, technology, and policy. Furthermore, understanding economic, political, and societal shifts has allowed my team and me to anticipate challenges and ensure that UJ remains relevant and forward-thinking.

Second, higher education leadership is evolving and it is apparent that traditional top-down models are giving way to more collaborative and adaptive approaches. I have been open to unconventional solutions to help create a dynamic and resilient institution. Leaders who encourage experimentation and adaptability position their universities for long-term success.

Last, I have prioritized investing in mentorship programs across the institution to help cultivate leadership at all levels. In addition to this, fostering a culture of trust and inclusivity has ensured that emerging leaders feel valued and engaged. In this vein, regularly engaging with stakeholders—including the students, faculty, staff, alumni, and broader community—has ensured alignment and shared vision.

Personal Identity and Perception

My life took a dramatic turn when I came across Kyokushin karate, which has informed me in much of my leadership journey. We were trained to fully appreciate the fact that the martial arts skills we possessed came with great responsibility. We had to exercise self-control to really master the art of this style of karate. A key lesson from this process was the act of mentorship.

We learned a set of principles that include training the body and heart to develop an unshakable spirit; pursuing the true meaning of the martial way; cultivating a spirit of self-denial, modesty, ambition, and serenity; keeping your head low, eyes high, and mouth shut; respecting your superiors and observing the rules of courtesy; practicing all of your knowledge without comparing yourself to others; persevering and having the strength to surpass obstacles without changing your mind; and finally, understanding that the true spirit of a karateka comes from applying karate in real life.

As I spent years honing my karate skills, I learned a great deal about discipline. Karate places a strong emphasis on discipline as a fundamental aspect of training. It provides a structured environment and a set of principles and practices that foster discipline. Karate training begins and ends with a series of rituals and etiquette, such as bowing to the instructor and fellow students.

These practices instill a sense of respect for oneself, the instructors, and the fellow practitioners. Respect for authority and others is a core component of discipline. Karate dojos often have a code of conduct that outlines expectations for behavior and attitude with a focus on values such as perseverance, self-control, and humility. Practitioners are expected to adhere to these principles by reinforcing discipline in their actions and interactions. Karate training follows a structured curriculum with a progressive system of belts or ranks. Advancing through the ranks requires dedication, consistent effort, and discipline.

The techniques learned must be executed with precision, and students must pay attention to details including body alignment, timing, and breathing. Through focused practice, students learn to control their minds and develop concentration skills, which are essential components of discipline. It was in the dojo that I found ways to manage my emotions, impulses, and reactions during training and sparring and—by virtue—in life.

These are tenets that I have carefully applied to my leadership approach. In particular, there are three interlinked concepts: persevering, trying, and not giving up. These ideas are reflected in my approach to my role and thus adequately outline perceptions of me. Furthermore—as I have alluded—my background and the parallels with the students of UJ have been an important factor in my leadership style. It is about understanding the significance of a degree for many from similar socioeconomic backgrounds.

Advice for Fellow Leaders

We have to lead with conviction. In this position, our vision must be clear and unwavering. Whether it's driving academic excellence, fostering inclusivity, or advancing research, we need to believe in our mission and communicate it effectively. A strong sense of purpose will not only inspire others but also help you stay grounded in the face of challenges.

Moreover, we have to remember that our constituency is the students. We must listen to them and incorporate them in decision-making structures. For instance, structures such as the UJ Student Representative Council (SRC) are imperative in bridging leadership gaps.

Our student leadership is a critical partner in tackling the enduring challenges pervading the sector. It is through the support of the SRC that we have been able to pivot tangible and lasting solutions for the student body. We have to remember that students are the heart of any institution. Their needs and challenges evolve, and staying attuned to them is crucial. It is imperative to create open channels for dialogue. Being present and accessible fosters trust and ensures that your leadership remains student-centered. Finally, I would encourage leaders to learn from their predecessors.

Past leaders have invaluable insights on the institution's history, culture, strengths, and—of course—challenges. Learning from their successes and their struggles is an important tool for navigating obstacles more effectively. While we all bring our own vision to the table, understanding past decisions can provide context and prevent the repetition of mistakes.

Similarly, your executive team, faculty administrative staff, and advisers are there to support and guide you. Trust their expertise, empower them to lead in their respective areas, and cultivate a culture of collaboration. Great leadership is not about having all the answers. Rather, it is about knowing who to turn to when you need them.

Guidance for Aspiring Leaders

At UJ, we have a unique approach to the transition and handover process. In the months after the announcement of my appointment as vice-chancellor in 2022, I stepped into the role of vice-chancellor designate and spent a great deal of time learning from Professor Marwala.

During this time, I began to get a real sense of the foundations and structures that make up the institution. Studies have found that leadership mentoring improves retention rates and job satisfaction.

Throughout my career, I have learned a great deal from mentors, and this has informed me in my leadership approach. With the collective support of my mentors, I was able to develop into the person, academic, and leader I am today. I am truly grateful for their mentorship, as I wouldn't have achieved what I have without them. To me, this is an important reminder that leaders do not emerge alone. I would encourage aspiring vice-chancellors to learn from those around them. This role is more than just a title—it carries the weight of shaping lives and even societies.

Every decision you make will have a ripple effect on the students, faculty, research, and broader community. It is important to approach this role with humility, to act with integrity, and to maintain a commitment to the long-term success of the institution.

Finally, from my own experience, you must think beyond day-to-day administration to leave a lasting mark. Advocate for policies that improve education accessibility, speak to sustainability, drive innovation, and strengthen the institution's legacy. Measure success not just in rankings but in how well your leadership uplifts individuals and communities.

Championing Diversity and Advancement

Since our inception, we have prioritized transformation as a strategic objective, leading to increased representation in leadership positions across academic and support divisions. The Black and women academic and research staff components, respectively, have increased to around 50 percent.

To further institutionalize these efforts, we established in 2019 a Gender Equity Unit, tasked with designing programs, providing professional support and training, implementing case management systems, and conducting research to monitor and evaluate gender-related initiatives.

The unit also addresses issues such as gender-based violence and discrimination, ensuring a comprehensive approach to gender equity. In 2020, we launched the Research Leadership Programme (RLP) to bolster the leadership skills of Black women researchers, accelerating their advancement toward becoming renowned scholars. The RLP offers mentorship and support.

Building on these initiatives, UJ unveiled the Women's Leadership Development Programme, which is dedicated to empowering senior women in academia and support functions. This program addresses persistent gender disparities, such as the gender pay gap, by equipping women with the necessary skills and support to excel in leadership roles. In conceptualizing this program, we knew all too well that part of our duty as an institution was to right these societal imbalances.

Importantly, this is a shift we need to be seeing in other facets of our society. We also knew that change could not be confined to corners of our institution but instead had to move the very structures and systems that allow for inequality to persist. Other initiatives aimed at transformation include the Accelerated Academic Mentorship Programme, which was designed to provide mentorship, support, development opportunities, and focused advice to a nominated group of permanent academic staff, thereby creating the conditions for these candidates to advance their academic career trajectories.

Similarly, the Future Professors Programme, spearheaded by the Department of Higher Education and Training and run at UJ, is aimed at developing the qualities of academic excellence and leadership in university scholarship. Both of these programs were conceptualized to be transformative for Black and women academics.

Conclusion

In conclusion, UJ's journey embodies a commitment to educational excellence, societal impact, and sustainability. As we navigate the complexities of the modern world, UJ remains dedicated to fostering a culture of innovation and inclusivity and ensuring that our graduates are not only equipped with knowledge but also inspired to effect positive changes in their communities.

Our collective vision for the future is rooted in ethical leadership and a deep understanding of our responsibilities to society that paves the way for a brighter, more equitable world for generations to come.

10 Turning Vision into Execution

Thandwa Zizwe Mthembu

Vice-Chancellor and Principal, Durban University of Technology (South Africa)

Introducing My Institution

The Durban University of Technology (DUT) is located on the warm east coast of South Africa in the province of KwaZulu-Natal (KZN). It sprawls over seven campuses that serve approximately 33,000 students. Two of these are in Pietermaritzburg, located within the spectacular KZN Midlands, an agricultural and tourism area well known for its green, undulating hills that unfurl eastward to the coast from the nearby Drakensberg Mountains. Five of these are in tropical and picturesque Durban, which sits ensconced beside the Valley of a Thousand Hills as it tapers off into the Indian Ocean.

DUT's establishment stems from a 2002–04 voluntary merger between the erstwhile ML Sultan Technikon and Technikon Natal. While the two institutions still stand in proximity in Durban, separated only by a road, they operated independently. Apartheid's (il)logic dictated that the former, which historically catered to Indian students, had to remain operationally distant from the latter, which catered to White students. That this merger—the first among public universities in South Africa—was voluntary in post-1994 South Africa is self-evident given the proximity and the illogic. The merger also involved the incorporation of the former Indumiso College of Education, based in Pietermaritzburg about eighty kilometers northwest of Durban; this became part of the KZN Midlands campuses.

Technikons offered rigid, work-focused, and vocational qualifications that were tailored to narrowly defined jobs as they emerged then from the job market. Pre-2002, a technikon was a postsecondary institution in South Africa—equivalent to a polytechnic institution in other parts of the world—that provided career-focused vocational training. Their enrollment peaked in the 1980s and 1990s, and they were very popular largely because the nature of the qualifications often led to immediate jobs just before and upon degree completion. As the job market changed in the twenty-first century, new job types emerged. Essentially, technikons could not keep up with the pace of change. Their qualifications had become rather hackneyed, and they thus failed to translate into the adaptable knowledge and skills that the new twenty-first century jobs—then in a state of flux—required. Between 2002 and 2004, technikons that were not merged with traditional universities became universities of technology. There were fifteen of them, reduced to only six after the mergers, and renamed universities of technology.

Even though mergers of South African public universities were not necessarily aimed at responding to the changing job environment, they provided an opportunity for universities of technology (UoTs) to think differently about the education they offered. From the predecessor institutions being rigid and vocationally focused, the first transition from technikons to UoTs involved the latter continuing to fashion themselves as higher education institutions that were educating and training for the workplace despite tectonic shifts in the workplace that had already ensued. Meanwhile, the disjuncture continued to widen with the twenty-first century job market expecting more versatility, agility, and adaptability.

It is this disjuncture that motivated DUT to innovate in 2019, leading to its ten-year values- and principles-based, outcomes- and impact-oriented, one-pager strategy map that one of our staff members called ENVISION2030, a name that was formally adopted. Its design follows the Balanced Scorecard, which was developed by Robert S. Kaplan and David P Norton in 1992. It is a strategic planning and management system used to communicate an organization's intent and translate its strategy into action. In the private and industrial sector, this normally consists of four financial and nonfinancial perspectives, namely financial, customer, internal process, and learning and growth. At DUT, we innovated and tailor-made our perspectives to fit the university environment. We presented our balanced scorecard as a strategy map, which is just a visual representation of the strategy that shows all of the interconnections among our strategic objectives.

Like many balanced scorecards, DUT's has four perspectives: stewardship, systems and processes, sustainability, and society. Each of these perspectives has three strategic objectives (SOs), and thus a total of twelve. As noted, it is outcomes- and impact-oriented, eschewing orientation toward inputs and outputs. It is also very much informed by research and data, having employed many research outcomes from many sources beyond Kaplan and Norton, some of which are revealed below.

The stewardship perspective has as its SOs: lived values, institutional culture, and creativity. These three SOs are predicated on a unique DUT DNA; its two strands are a people-centered and engaged mindset and an innovative and entrepreneurial approach. The base pairs that connect the two strands consist of five values (transparency, honesty, respect, integrity, and accountability), and five principles (fairness, professionalism, commitment, compassion, and excellence).

While it would take many pages to delve into the rest of the perspectives that focus on the nexus of teaching-learning, research-innovation, and engagement, what DUT ultimately wishes to achieve is to make contributions that help to improve the lives and the livelihoods of society at large. Through creativity, innovation, and entrepreneurship, we are focused on transforming our society and its economy. As a university, we will achieve this through our new DUT philosophy of education statement: "Our creativity and innovation shapes adaptive graduates who transform society."

This philosophy will catapult the education DUT offers. No longer shall DUT be educating and training for a workplace that is in flux and ephemeral, but it will produce agile, versatile, and adaptive graduates who will transform society and its economy. In short, this philosophy is constructivist, creative, innovative, and outcomes- and impact-oriented.

I hasten to point out that monitoring and evaluating outcomes and impact is a hard slog. Neither do our staff and stakeholders nor the governing bodies and structures we report to fully understand and appreciate this approach. We could not either when we started, and we are still learning. Our national and institutional systems also do not have appropriate key performance indicators (KPIs), measures and targets, several of which we had to devise from scratch. They are still stuck in the inputs-outputs paradigm. As a simple example, it is much easier to count research outputs in high-impact journals than to assess their local and regional impact.

Leadership Tenure

The year 2025 marks my nineteenth year in the position of vice-chancellor and principal (often referred to as rector or president in other jurisdictions); I am one of the longest-serving vice-chancellors in a South African public university. I started out in January 2007 at the Central University of Technology, Free State (CUT) and in October 2016 moved to DUT.

At both CUT and DUT I was able to organically develop ten-year strategies, which I began to implement doggedly, with very little room to brook prevarication and dissent. At CUT it was Vision 2020, and at DUT it is ENVISION2030. South Africa's management system tends to encourage five-year strategies, missions, and visions. We bucked this trend and expectation by producing an ENVISION2030 strategy with a ten-year horizon only a statement of intent, with perspectives, strategic objectives, and logic interweaving everything to what we promise to society.

At CUT—and to some extent at DUT, too—so many stakeholders and structures of governance bought into the strategy and began to assist in the implementation processes. At CUT, even unions fully understood and advocated for the strategy and its implications to influence what they would demand from management. Sometimes, the unionists' rhetoric on advocating for the strategy would sound much better than some of our executives. This is the extent to which the use-case model—a constructivist model allowing different types of people for whom something is being conceived or created to be part of devising a solution for it—could entrench ownership.

At DUT, there remains serious inertia, most probably because of its pre-1994 apartheid moorings that are difficult to shake. However, many staff, students, and alumni remain excited about what DUT has achieved over the past five years since ENVISION2030 was adopted and ushered in. Several new recruits claim to have been drawn to DUT by this vision. Granted, some are disappointed by the inertia they experience, which seeks to keep DUT stagnant or retrogressive. This is our new challenge.

Professional Journey

It helped a lot that I come from a family where excellence in general was taken for granted. Education—and doing well in it—was nonnegotiable. It is no wonder that we have three PhDs in our family of five siblings, with two more PhDs in the generation after us. My wife and her sister also have PhDs.

Both my mother and father were stern teachers who taught me formally in two of my primary school classes. As I moved from primary to secondary school, my father's former student happened to be our mathematics and science teacher and principal. I had no choice but to excel in mathematics and science.

Completing my thesis in mathematics—more specifically, in weighted polynomial approximation theory—at the age of twenty-seven and graduating a year later gave me a great advantage in our sector. Many people still think that if you are a mathematician, you are a genius and can do just about anything. So, I found myself entrusted with many leadership tasks and roles, including nonmathematical and nonacademic ones.

In 1994, South Africa ushered in a new democracy, which came with lots of opportunities and challenges, too. Not only did I take advantage of opportunities in a new democracy to grow in academic leadership, but some of the challenges I was foolhardy enough to tackle also catapulted my career. In my early thirties, about six years after earning my PhD, I became an associate professor at a small university campus and the head of its mathematics department.

In nonacademic and broader institutional transformative matters, I got deeply involved in the leadership of the then-used broad transformation forums, which were multi-stakeholder forums that focused on change and transformation in all facets of university life as the new democracy took shape. Many ideas were needed to reimagine and reshape the university both academically and administratively. While I may not have been popular with higher education executives of the time because of my activism—and I was branded persona non grata at some stage—it appears that many people appreciated the transformative roles I had been playing.

With soaring academic and nonacademic influences, I was entrusted with even more serious leadership functions that further enhanced my professional journey. By the age of thirty-seven, I had become a deputy vice-chancellor at the erstwhile University of Durban-Westville, now part of the University of KwaZulu-Natal. Two years later, in 2002, I was back at Wits for my second deputy vice-chancellorship.

I have a little anecdote about my return to Wits. On graduating with a PhD about eleven years earlier, I had told some friends and colleagues that I would return and occupy a senior-level position. This is exactly what happened. One of my older friends, the late Mr. Enock Zulu—a fellow villager and a security officer at Wits—kept asking me where I got my magic wand!

Distinct Contributions to Leadership

My predecessors did a lot to transform and extricate DUT from an overwhelmingly technikon culture and practice that was not much different from one at a glorified high school. But, with great effort, DUT soon changed to befit the name of university. Given how difficult it is to change institutional culture, this continues to be work in progress even today. As is often attributed to management consultant Peter Drucker, culture eats strategy for breakfast; this occurs through inertia and other subcultural ills. It has been my experience at DUT, and it continues to be a great challenge.

Our unique approach to change and transformation has several aspects that I deem important not only for DUT but for any university anywhere in the world.

- Vision: DUT produced ENVISION2030—a values- and principles-based, outcomes- and impact-oriented strategy— which was a great milestone. ENVISION2030 focuses on our broader society and moves away from siloed input- and output-based approaches that are largely narcissistic for a university.
- Impact: DUT benefitted from focusing more on not just producing a novel strategy but rather identifying new impact-oriented KPIs, measures, and targets for implementing it—and doing so doggedly, despite inertia from some quarters that are hell-bent on returning to a past long gone.
- Visible change: Physically, academically, and substantively, no one can miss that DUT is different, upending, and transforming (the latter three words being a creative play on the initialism DUT). While our physical infrastructure had remained dilapidated for years, a new look for DUT—both in Durban and Pietermaritzburg—has already emerged.
- Rankings: While I am personally not a fan of rankings, circumstances at DUT and beyond led us to them—or, rather, we unavoidably found ourselves in them. In international rankings, DUT has improved its position remarkably. Nationally, it is placed first amongst all UoTs based on several outputs and impacts.
- Brand-new education: DUT is the first among UoTs to not only craft a unique philosophy of education but to also begin to implement it using project-based learning, design thinking and many other constructivist approaches. Yes, other universities may well be employing these learning strategies, but they may do so without necessarily jettisoning the old and hackneyed approaches.
- Transformation: Even though we have not yet reached this milestone, our academic structure will transform to align with DUT's new philosophy of education. Very few universities in our country have had a thorough review of their institutional arrangements and curricula beyond aligning to requirements of accrediting bodies.

I believe that I have made more tangential contributions to the sector, which arose naturally during my tenure and from which a variety of lessons could be learned.

- Stay academic: Once an academic system and its subsystems have been put in place, the university must be run accordingly. Of course, there will be necessary refinements, reviews, and changes along the way. But, based on the existing system, facts, evidence, reason, and debate must reign supreme and must also be seen to be reigning supreme. Pretense to politics—petty or hard expediency and opportunism, including attempts at celebrity status—are inimical to being academic or being an academic manager.
- Keep copious records: In 2012–13 and now recently in 2023–24, I found myself being accused falsely by my detractors to a point that the allegations were without merit and my dismissal was moot on both occasions. But undoubtedly, I have been the comeback kid—twice. The first incident was at the level of the then-minister, which was roundly defeated at the relevant High Court of South Africa via a more than 1,000-page affidavit that I had written based on facts and evidence collected over the years. The most recent one was at the level of our governing body, the Council. The Council had become divided and fraught, with some of the members frustrated at not getting financial benefits in university tenders. They had wrongly assumed that I would support these undeserved and corrupt benefits, which they seemed to have forgotten was not allowed by the system they put in place. An urgent application at the High Court in September 2024 stopped them dead in their tracks, with personal costs to them.
- Winnow the many stories: Many people, both internal and external, will either tell true stories or make them up for some benefit. Some of those may date back to many years and may have been argued away definitively. But with a new person in the job, some will think they could make their cases winnable to that person. Do not take anything at face value. Take no prisoners in pursuit of your values and principles. Winnow and wind-tunnel every detail against facts and evidence, reason and debate, and the overall system in place.
- When days are dark friends are few: This proverb is also the title of a song by the late Sipho Gumede, a South African bass guitarist and contemporary jazz maestro. Those very close to me know it very well. What a surprise to know that some of those who confess and appear to be close to you have their own agendas, including those that could bump you out. At CUT, when someone I had been mentoring for

many years and another one who had not been wanted by anyone, (but I had managed to convince council to accept), chose to align with my detractors in the 2012–13 debacle, I was dumbfounded, to say the least. At DUT, several internal people, including some I could never have imagined, fueled the latest debacle out of their own misguided suspicions. During these debacles, not even a handful of my colleagues in the sector ever called to empathize with me until they learned I had won.

- It is cold and lonely at the top: Sometimes, being at the top makes some think they are self-sufficient and beyond education and advice. There are many who have walked your path and could advise and turn your adversity into success.
- Ability and aptitude versus character and attitude: The late John Wooden, an American basketball coach, said, "Ability may take you to the top, but it takes character to keep you there" (Wooden, n.d.). I was rather rebellious and cantankerous during the earlier stages of my professional life. As I said earlier, I was at some stage persona non grata in the university sector. It is my alma mater, Wits, that saved me by giving me space to reflect and build a different character. Professors Norma Reid and Loyiso Nongxa, two successive vice-chancellors of Wits between 2002 and 2007, made this possible. I was pleasantly surprised when I was described as thoughtful, calm, and a keen listener after assuming the role of deputy vice-chancellor there in 2002.

Effective Leadership Strategies

There is obviously not one working strategy for effective leadership. My inspiration has been drawn from erudite friends and family, and most importantly, several management gurus and authors such as Peter Drucker, Jim Collins, and others—too many to mention. Below are a few leadership strategies I have gleaned from all these coveted authors and have employed successfully.

- Inspiration and motivation: I mention Peter Drucker and Jim Collins specifically because there are many of their gems I employ to motivate our people. For example, Jim Collins's book *Good to Great: Why Some Companies Make the Leap … and Others Don't* allowed me to argue that being good makes one rest on one's laurels. Meanwhile, your competition would be honing its skills to beat you at your game and becoming great while you remain good; hence, as Collins stated, "good is the enemy of great" (Collins 2001, 1). We have also branded the DUT people who are enthusiastic about our strategy as the right people who are occupying the right seats, performing their functions right, and ultimately, doing the right things and doing them right. The latter part of the sentence is obviously inspired by the famous quotation that "management is doing things right; leadership is doing the right things," which is commonly attributed to Peter Drucker.

- Viable systems model (VSM): This world is a VUCA (volatility, uncertainty, complexity, and ambiguity) world, which requires agility, versatility and adaptiveness, amongst many values and principles. VSM is simply a model that helps one to think of, and operate in, an organization as if it were an interdependent network of autonomous systems, such as a neural network. At the outset, I must acknowledge my brother, Ntokozo Mthembu, PhD, who introduced me to VSM—and cybernetics in particular—more than twenty years ago when completing his PhD on this topic. Many readings by Stafford Beer, its founder, and other authors in cybernetics have helped to grow my interest and knowledge in this field, without being an expert in it. Since then, I have used this theoretical approach as a broad conceptual framework for my work. Of course, it does help that by training I am a mathematician—a field that forces order, structure, generalization, and deconstruction.
- Research-informed, creative, and innovative: Whatever one conceptualizes, designs, plans, and executes as a manager, especially in a university environment where research is part of the core business, must be research-informed. This is demonstrated by our liberal employment of many concepts from several authors in ENVISION2030. What is all the existing research in management for if it is not applicable and useful in a university setting? This approach also allows for innovation by the reader, as demonstrated in the first bullet.
- Use-case model: No chief executive officer (in our case, a vice-chancellor) could lead only based on the depth of their knowledge and skills. There is, unfortunately, an inverse relationship between higher levels of knowledge and experience, on the one hand, and the deficit-based model on the other hand. A deficit-based model is a

model that attributes perceived failures in solving a particular problem as a lack of knowledge, skills, achievement, and learning. It relates more to a top-down approach in the assumption that people at lower levels have very little to offer. Organically, we often employ the use-case model in lots of what we have achieved. It provides much better ownership especially when tough aspects of a strategy must be implemented. While this model is preferred, there may be situations that instead require a deficit-based model. The right choices must be made carefully when each one is employed.

- The surrogate, midwife, and nanny leader/manager: About two years ago, I had a discussion with my direct reports on my leadership style, and the childbearing and child-caring analogy just came out organically. One of the executives said I am like a surrogate mother who carries babies (projects) for other executives even though they have been employed and are well paid to carry them to full term. Another said he thinks I am a midwife, in that I am the one conceiving ideas in all sorts of fields while there are executives who could do so on their own if they focused. I had so far thought that I had only been a nanny, taking care of my executives' projects and suggesting solutions when there were challenges.
- Focus on strategy and implementation: Once a strategy has been crafted, it cannot just be put on the shelves. One thing people say South African managers and leaders are good at is devising strategies and policies. Yet after all that, very few implement anything, often remaining stuck in ideology and general inaction; to avoid this, we made sure to put implementation systems in place. We must be both good leaders and good managers. Once we have done the right things, we must do them right. Just a short anecdote to share about relentless implementation: After almost ten years of filibustering by our unions since 2008, in 2018 we introduced our performance management system (PMS). As of 2023, an electronically run PMS is in place, with over 80 percent of our staff participating in it. Part of this system consists of a 360-degree behavioral evaluation designed to assess whether people live out the values and principles we introduced previously.
- Incremental progress, as discussed in *Atomic Habits: An Easy & Proven Way to Build Good Habits & Break Bad Ones* by James Clear (2018), suggests small habitual steps could eventually lead to a complete

cultural change. While detractors may criticize a strategic focus amid some nagging dysfunction at some lower levels, nothing beats focusing and inspiring one's people strategically, systemically, and systematically. It is the surest way of making progress despite whatever inertia. Ultimately, VSM is about building systems and subsystems and getting them networked. While so many irritations in our systems and processes could be pointed to, a different, upending, and transforming DUT cannot be contradicted. Just one anecdote in this regard: With much resistance from unions as alluded to previously, the PMS that I referred to was introduced incrementally over the past five years. Warts and all, many see it as helping them to focus on their primary work and its impact.

Personal Identity and Perception

When I became aware of my existence as a human being, I found myself out in the field looking after my extended family's stock—cattle and sheep. Only two boys had been born in the extended family in the 1960s. Our birth a few months apart had brought so much joy to our older cousins, as they later revealed. They would soon be excused from this chore. In fact, I had already been enrolled for my very first year of school when a debate ensued in my extended family about who would look after the family stock while I was attending school. That was the end of my school sojourn. It took my nuclear family's move elsewhere far away from my extended family compound for me to start school the following year.

As noted, I was raised by very stern parents who were teachers. My father was a strict and pedantic primary school principal. I learned a lot from him, and I understand that I exhibit some of his leadership traits.

There are just two anecdotes on self-agency and self-bureaucracy on the one hand and integrity on the other, which I took out of a lifetime of lessons from my parents. I must have been about twelve years of age when they left home on a Saturday for a function. For us, their absence was a field day of fun. They returned in the late afternoon. Lo and behold, my father asked me to give an account of what I had accomplished that day. When I started to argue that he had not given me any specific instruction, I got a big hiding for having been loitering and aimless the entire day. My mother just nodded affirmatively, providing no solace. According to them, amid so many glaring chores in the homestead, I did not have to be reminded what it is I could have done without being told to do. I had been old enough and well accustomed to what could possibly be done. In retrospect, that episode left indelible lessons on self-agency and self-bureaucracy.

My father would also prepare some financial statements on charts to display at a school governing body or a parents' meeting. Our job was to transcribe these statements and notes from some exercise book he had written them on. The handwriting had to be meticulous, mimicking his. He also taught us calligraphic writing, which we used to embellish the writing on the charts. During registration time, the fees for which were nominal, he would count every cent the parents had paid. And, if any cent had been missing, it would be war on us until it was found. His sense of integrity by safeguarding the school funds and taking his reports so seriously remains indelible in my whole being.

I also come from a deeply Christian family, which is not flaunted. About 130 years ago—in 1894—my family produced the first Black priest of an Anglican church in Zululand, KwaZulu-Natal, in Reverend Titus Mthembu, my great-grand uncle. My grandfather, Reverend Gideon Mthembu, qualified as a priest in 1921. My father, Thokoza Mthembu, completed his training in priesthood in 1967 amid his teaching career. My elder brother, Dr. Delani Mthembu, is a practicing priest. It is just unfortunate that many Christians have low regard for the unassailable power of the Holy Spirit, which Jesus left with us to guide our lives and use to tap into God's kingdom.

Educationally, I have also been influenced by my parents and aunts as a family of teachers. With many of my uncles having earned bachelor of science degrees in the 1950s at the University of Fort Hare, I could not have grown to be anything other than a mathematician or a scientist nor be educated other than through the same university. My mind works scientifically or mathematically, while I also have an artistic bent, being my family's lay historian and praise-singer. Unlike many who may see a distinction between science and Christianity, I do not.

Studying for a master's degree at Vanderbilt University in Nashville, Tennessee, and doing some summer courses at the University of Michigan in Ann Arbor, Michigan, during the late 1980s provided me with lessons on self-directed learning and the enormity of brain capacity. A thick textbook would be imbibed in a flash, largely with one's own self-agency! Studying and working at the University of the Witwatersrand (Wits) in Johannesburg during my PhD days gave me a perspective to academic excellence that has since remained with me. I will use an anecdote to illustrate this.

Between the two semesters in an academic year, there is a three-week break in June to July in the southern academic calendar. In my first year of teaching at Wits, I was quite excited to visit my village of Nkandla during this break. On my return, a fellow postgraduate student—now-retired Professor Kathy Driver—welcomed me to some stunning results she had produced during the break on hypergeometric functions. Embarrassingly, I had absolutely no research results to report. That was the last time I took an academic break for a social break!

Leadership Style and Perceptions of It

I am confident that perceptions of my management and leadership styles emanate from a complex mix of influences, most provided previously—not least from my social and religious backgrounds, my stern parents, my school principal father, but they also stem from my scientific and mathematical training at the University of Fort Hare, in the US, and at Wits and my leadership experiences over the rest of my professional career.

I could be a little jollier and exuberant in personality, I admit. But I am my rather demure, pensive, and inscrutable parents' son. Notwithstanding, I believe my leadership is open and predictable because my values and principles are clear and consistent. I believe I am so transparent that anyone who approaches me for a decision or an opinion should already know what the answer is going to be. Admittedly, this could certainly make those around me feel that I am overly pedantic and rigid when some political malleability could sometimes be appropriate. Well, my view is that one is only an academic; it is difficult to become a petty politician in a university environment.

Championing Diversity and Advancement

There is nothing as useful and as progressive as putting the university's resources and positions where your mouth is. During most of my first term at DUT (2016–21), two of my three deputy vice-chancellors were women, including the registrar. Between 2020 and 2024, our chief financial officer was also a woman. In their unique ways, they certainly brought different perspectives to the table, which made my work easier. Being male with lots of natural blind spots on matters female, I had several women who provided advice and drove transformation in several areas.

At DUT, though, we have a different challenge regarding diversity. DUT's challenge, rather, is with respect to representation and equity among Indians, Colored, White, and Africans, as our racial classifications go. These classifications have remained long after the apartheid system disappeared, ostensibly (and ironically) to create equality. It remains that the Africans who were the most politically, socially, and economically oppressed during apartheid are the ones who remain less represented.

Indians constitute only about 3 percent in the country but about 9 percent in KwaZulu-Natal, where most of the population is located (Statistics South Africa 2023). However, at DUT, according to KZN's Economically Active Population, Indians constitute about three times their share while Africans compose about half of the level of their representation.

With more than 90 percent of our students and staff being African, they are not a minority but rather the overwhelming majority. Over the years, we have seen enrollments of White students declining drastically. Of course, with about 7 percent of the entire South African population being White people (Statistics South Africa 2023), we could not expect high numbers of White students at DUT. However, if we are to be true to equity, we must now strive to address the dismally low enrollment of our young White people.

Since the two constituent technikons were White and Indian, for some reason, Indians preponderated. As a result, Africans tend to be concentrated mostly at the top and bottom levels, while Indians are largely represented in the middle tier. This distribution makes it difficult for many Africans, especially those in lower positions, to see themselves reflected in the middle levels of the institution. For some strange reason, even those who are being empowered in our transformation journey do not seem to appreciate it.

References

Clear, James. 2018. *Atomic Habits: An Easy & Proven Way to Build Good Habits & Break Bad Ones*. Avery.

Collins, Jim. 2001. *Good to Great: Why Some Companies Make the Leap … And Others Don't*. Harper Business.

Statistics South Africa. 2023. *Census 2022 Statistical Release: P0301.4 Population Group Distribution by Province in South Africa, 1996-2022*. Statistics South Africa.

Wooden, John. n.d. "Motivational Quotes." https://www.thewoodeneffect.com/motivational-quotes/.

11 From Vision to Collective Action

Edward Peck

Vice-Chancellor and President, Nottingham Trent University (United Kingdom)

Introducing My Institution

Granted university status in 1992, Ncttingham Trent University (NTU) traces its origins to 1843 with the creation of the Nottingham Government School of Design. This makes it one of the longest-established institutions in England that provides education to adults. Its key purposes—driving innovation and developing skills—are deeply embedded in its past, its present, and its future.

Alongside this original close connection with business have grown two other areas of focus: to enable people to change their life opportunities through education and to partner with local civic organizations in strengthening the local communities and the services on which they depend.

NTU is among the ten largest universities in the UK, with almost 4,500 staff, more than 37,000 students, and an annual income of approximately £400 million. NTU has five campuses across Nottingham and Nottinghamshire and one in London, each distinguished by its subject mix and distinctive student population.

NTU has been given numerous awards: *The Times* and *The Sunday Times* Modern University of the Year 2023 and 2018, Whatuni Student Choice Awards University of the Year 2023, *Guardian* University Awards University of the Year 2019, and *Times Higher Education* Awards University of the Year 2017. It has ascended the major international league tables and has been placed second on a global sustainability ranking for several years in succession.

It has received gold—the highest-level recognition in the Teaching Excellence Framework—on both occasions that the UK's Office for Students has conducted a national review of student experience and outcomes, most recently in 2024. In 2021, it was the most improved institution in the Research Excellence Framework, the UK's peer assessment of the quality of research outputs, environment, and impact.

The current university strategy—University, reimagined—expresses in six word pairs (or twelve words) our shared ambitions of creating opportunity, valuing ideas, enriching society, embracing sustainability, connecting globally, and empowering people. NTU has also adopted three key principles that guide the decision-making of colleagues across the institution: We change lives; we are bold; and we do the right thing.

Our current priority is to undertake the next strategic process in the context of five key factors that we think will shape universities over the next decade, all of which are in flux: the influence of AI; the expectations of students; the concerns of society; the nature of graduate work; and the changing demographic of students. These issues are also influencing government policy in England that addresses higher education; the next institutional strategy will also need to respond to the UK government's position on immigration up to 2030. Finally, the financial context for NTU—whilst still positive in comparison with most other higher education providers in the UK and, indeed, those around the world—may constrain some of the options available or, at least, the extent to which they can be developed and implemented.

Leadership Tenure

I joined NTU as vice-chancellor and president in 2014. It was a good institution, with some outstanding infrastructure, but it had lost touch with what it was trying to achieve. Twenty years on from being granted university status, this lack of clear purpose had undermined its ability to create a sense of confidence and pride.

As a result, developing the first strategy on my watch—Creating the University of the Future 2015–20—became an exercise in addressing what I believe to be one of the foundational truths of organizational life: "Where there is no vision, the people perish" (Proverbs 29:18). This required an inclusive and engaging strategy process, which generated the two areas of focus and the six word pairs that articulate our shared ambitions. This approach was repeated in our more recent strategy development process, which resulted in University, reimagined 2020–25.

At the same time, in my view there is another foundational truth. To misquote slightly the English painter and poet William Blake, they who would do good must do so in small particulars. It is in the everyday actions of colleagues across NTU that strategy is enacted. One of my own aphorisms—with which those who work at NTU will be perhaps overly familiar—asserts that strategy is what people do, not what other people write down.

Looking back, mobilizing the energy of colleagues in support of a vision that drove demonstrable change and that we had shaped and owned together was the defining moment of my tenure. It was then that I felt that my presence as the leader of NTU was a good fit for both the institution and for me.

I will be stepping down from the role this summer as part of a long-standing succession plan. This chapter is thus a timely opportunity to reflect on my eleven years at the helm.

Professional Journey

My first degree was in philosophy and in my subsequent studies I moved toward organizational sociology. Before I ceased to be an active academic, I was researching, writing, teaching, and consulting in organizational development and institutional leadership. Becoming vice-chancellor was an opportunity for me to apply some of my theoretical ideas in practice. I shall return to this topic in the next section.

However, my first career was in the UK's National Health Service. I joined as a National Management Graduate Trainee, an equivalent scheme to the fast-track route into the UK Civil Service. As a public servant, I see my role as being to prioritize the interests of those who use our services, whether they are patients or students. These interests should wherever possible take precedence over those of the institutions through which they may at present be delivered.

I spent twenty years working as a manager and consultant in and around health and social care. This means that I was a senior manager before I was a senior academic; most vice-chancellors and presidents have a professional journey that unfolds the other way around. When I took my first academic role, I was appointed simultaneously as a head of an academic department—so even then I was viewing my contribution, at least in part, through a managerial lens.

I had a lot to learn about the culture and structure of higher education as well as its policy and practice. It took me twelve years from that first role—through further promotions—before I was appointed vice-chancellor at NTU.

Distinct Contributions to Leadership

It was perhaps inevitable that my unusual combination of practical experiences and academic insights has made my contributions distinctive, and, in some respects, unique, in contemporary UK higher education. I will articulate just a few connected examples.

I previously noted my perspective that the purpose of strategy is to mobilize the commitment of colleagues to deliver practical actions that will achieve our shared ambitions. At the same time, there is little benefit in mobilizing the commitment of colleagues who are not good at what the institution requires them to do. As a result, NTU has implemented what I believe to be the most rigorous appraisal system in the sector, complete with individual performance ratings. These can carry financial consequences that are mostly positive, such as bonuses; this is not always the case, for example, if objectives are not met.

There is much written in the organizational literature about the importance of culture and strategy with which I agree. However, there is less focus on structure, by which I mean in this context the crucial role that accountability exercised through line management plays. The setting and monitoring of objectives for individuals sends a clear message about what is valued—in one sense, quite literally—by NTU. The benefit of this approach can be seen in the results from the annual National Student Survey. In most years, NTU scores well above the average across all categories of questions and, more relevant to this point, does so with remarkable consistency across subjects, departments, and sites.

In parallel with this appraisal approach, NTU made the decision to leave national collective pay bargaining, in which all but a small handful of UK universities participate. One of the major benefits from this decision is that it allows NTU to align all elements of its reward package during negotiations with our trade unions: pay increase, progression up the pay spine, annual leave allowance, one-off payments, et cetera. In part as a consequence, NTU has not had any disruption due to strikes or other forms of industrial action since I joined; this record is genuinely unique in UK higher education.

Effective Leadership Strategies

I hope my leadership strategy is becoming clear: agree on our vision, articulate our ambitions, mobilize our colleagues' commitment, set our broad objectives, and review our individual and collective performance.

Once this approach was embedded—and it took three years to do so—even I was surprised at the growth in confidence and pride that ensued; this was both enhanced and exemplified by our first University of the Year award in 2017. Many more colleagues now take the initiative to innovate within their areas without feeling the need to seek permission. The best recent example is the introduction of relaxed graduation ceremonies in which neurodiverse graduates can choose to design a personalized approach that will meet their particular individual needs; again, these were the first of their kind in the country.

Personal Identity and Perception

I have written books about my perspective of leadership as performance, so I will not repeat the full argument. However, I want to be clear from the outset: Whilst there are overlaps, performing a role in an organization is most definitely not the same as performing a role in a play.

Most of all, this view of leadership calls for discipline. The greatest potential strength of organizational leaders is that everything done or said will be interpreted through the eyes of colleagues. At the same time, the greatest potential weakness of organizational leaders is that everything done or said will be interpreted through the eyes of colleagues.

It is incumbent upon us to judge in each situation the most constructive intervention that is in our repertoire and to work to extend this repertoire as we grow more experienced. Contrary to what some managerial gurus claim, being yourself is not enough; what may be enough is being the most effective version of yourself that you can conjure in the circumstances you find yourself in.

There are normally two challenges to this view. The first is that we all possess an essential self that is consistent, regardless of context. Well, I am not sure I see one revealed across my various roles as parent, grandparent, hockey umpire, charity trustee, hobby farmer, football supporter, and so on; rather, I draw upon my repertoire as seems most fitting to the activity, albeit on occasions with less discipline than I hope I show as vice-chancellor.

The second is that my approach will not make people feel that I am behaving with authenticity or integrity. My response is that most virtues attributed to a leader are just that—attributional; like beauty, they are in the eyes of the beholder. My argument is that colleagues see authenticity and integrity in my typically calm and measured approach as I seek to do the best for them and those we serve.

Advice for Fellow Leaders

I would offer humbly two suggestions to address the major challenges that faced me when I became vice-chancellor.

The first is the challenge of leading at a distance. The number of colleagues who are looking to you for leadership will multiply, in most cases many times, when you take up this role. You can only have the opportunity to create a personal relationship with a small subset. What I have learned is that colleagues want to have a feeling of affiliation—to find something shared that can form the basis of a conversation. As I did earlier in this chapter, I have introduced into the NTU community facts about myself that I hope will create some connection with all of my colleagues: I have two daughters and two young grandchildren; I support Everton Football Club; I keep sheep … you will see the point.

The second is the challenge of understanding the much bigger landscape that opens up to you suddenly after your appointment, some of which you might not realize at first is either there or that matters. It took me a while—as well as several conversations with a wide range of my own university colleagues and external partners—to become aware of the major gaps in my repertoire that I needed to overcome.

In my case, these areas were the most effective method of promoting NTU through effective public affairs and the best routes into the networks of influential people across our region. To deal with the first, the university appointed a specialist consultant, who over the next seven years enabled me to transform the profile and influence of NTU with national politicians, policymakers, and media; he is himself now a governor at NTU. For the second, we identified a new chancellor who was already affiliated with NTU, alongside being one of the most widely respected and well-connected individuals in our part of the UK.

Guidance for Aspiring Leaders

My main piece of advice for aspiring leaders is to curate your curriculum vitae; what got you here will not get you there. Talk to people who shape the perceptions of who is ready to be promoted to more senior roles in universities—in the UK, this is a small number of recruitment consultancies—about the strengths and weaknesses in your experience and expertise to date. Where possible, access people who have a reputation in the sector for being good at those things where you need to learn. This may mean working for them or asking them to be your mentor.

In my case, the weakness in my curriculum vitae was my lack of insight into the policy and practice of higher education and the cultural assumptions that shaped them. I was fortunate that I spent six years working for a vice-chancellor who was steeped in these issues and shared this broader wisdom during discussions on many topics that were considered by the senior team.

Championing Diversity and Advancement

We must demonstrate the importance that we attach to championing equality, diversity, and inclusion not just by what we say but by what we do. This has to be one of the top priorities for every senior leader.

Within Inclusion in Action—NTU's equity, diversity, and inclusion action plan—are three initiatives for which I take personal responsibility. The first is offering to be a mentor to academics from Black and ethnic minority backgrounds who are considering applying for promotion to professor. The second is exploring local plans and recent progress, including looking at key metrics, in depth during my annual reviews of every professional service department and academic school.

Thirdly, for the last four years I have chaired the University Shadow Executive Team (USET); I believe this to be unique in the UK. This group consists of around twenty individuals who have a range of protected characteristics under UK law; they are drawn from the same areas of responsibility as the members of the Extended University Executive Team (EUET). USET receives the same papers and briefings as EUET, and it brings a powerful set of voices and perspectives to the leadership and management of NTU that would otherwise not be heard so clearly and loudly.

Conclusion

As I prepare to leave my full-time career, I feel privileged to have worked for the National Health Service—the British institution of which the British public are most proud—and UK higher education, which I would contend is the aspect of the UK of which people around the world are most envious. The reputation of both is well founded in their achievements over many decades.

However, the impact of the five factors that I identified in the first section may well be profound over the next ten years. The response of universities has to be proportionate to this challenge. The responsibility of leaders may be to design and deliver significant change in a situation where the best guide to the future may not be the past. It will require them to question long-held practices and beliefs within institutions to an extent that may appear unreasonable. Then again, as I have heard said and taken to saying: If you want something to change, get someone unreasonable to do it.

12 A Visionary Approach to Institutional Transformation

Kakha Shengelia

President, Caucasus University (Georgia)

Introducing My Institution

Caucasus University (CU) is more than just an educational institution—it is a transformative force in the Caucasus region and beyond. Founded in 1998 with the support of the US Department of State and in collaboration with Georgia State University, CU has grown into a globally recognized hub of academic excellence and innovation. Its mission, "knowledge is a foundation of freedom," encapsulates its commitment to preparing highly qualified, ethically grounded professionals who are equipped to thrive in both local and international markets. By promoting critical thinking, ethical decision-making, and personal responsibility, CU fosters an environment in which students are empowered to become independent, thoughtful leaders in their fields. Through research-oriented teaching and learning, CU also fosters democratic ideals and meets society's evolving educational needs.

What sets CU apart is its unique blend of tradition and modernity. The university's historical roots are deeply intertwined with its global outlook. With campuses in Tbilisi, the capital of Georgia, and Batumi, on the Black Sea coast, as well as international partnerships spanning Europe and the US, CU offers students a truly global education. For almost fifteen years, CU has been designated as an off-site campus of Grenoble Ecole de Management and run one of the top-ranked executive master of business administration programs for Georgian and international students, which is currently ranked forty-seventh globally by the *Financial Times*. Additionally, CU has established its European campus in France, on the premises of Rennes School of Business, and an international training center in Dubai, United Arab Emirates.

CU has also brought the Basque Culinary Center to Georgia and is in the process of establishing the Basque Culinary Academy in Gurjaani—located within Georgia's renowned wine region—as a top-tier institution. This academy not only focuses on traditional culinary techniques but also emphasizes innovation, promotes sustainability, and prepares students to excel in the global food industry. This collaboration, along with others, reflects CU's commitment to providing students with unparalleled access to world-class business and specialized education—without leaving the region.

CU's commitment to excellence is further evidenced by its prestigious accreditations and rankings. The university holds the United Nations World Tourism Organization TedQual accreditation for its tourism programs as well as the Royal Institute of British Architects accreditation from the UK for its architecture program. It is the only university in the Caucasus region in the final stages of achieving Association to Advance Collegiate Schools of Business accreditation, the gold standard for business schools worldwide. These accreditations and rankings are not just badges of honor; they are a testament to CU's rigorous academic standards, innovative teaching methods, and strong commitment to student success.

With over fifty-seven bachelor's, master's, and doctoral programs spanning disciplines such as business, law, media, technology, architecture, governance, humanities and social sciences, tourism, medicine, economics, and education, CU is a hub of intellectual diversity. Its emphasis on research and innovation is evident in groundbreaking projects in cybersecurity, healthcare management, and social sciences that are supported by international donors such as the European Commission, the United Nations, and the US Agency for International Development. These research initiatives not only contribute to global knowledge but also provide students with opportunities to engage in cutting-edge projects that address real-world challenges.

CU's outstanding achievements include a 98 percent employment rate among graduates, partnerships with over 300 international universities, twelve double-degree programs with top universities in the US and Europe, 100 exchange agreements worldwide, the highest number of funded mobilities under the Erasmus+ program, and 25 percent of the student body consisting of international students from fifty-one different countries. These accomplishments underscore CU's role as a gateway to global opportunities for its students. CU graduates are highly sought after by employers, thanks to the university's emphasis on practical skills, critical thinking, and global awareness.

Leadership Tenure and Transformative Vision

My journey at Caucasus University began in 2000 when I became the dean of the Caucasus School of Business, and my visionary leadership ultimately led me to become the owner and president of the university in 2004. Over the course of my tenure, I guided the institution through a period of unprecedented growth and innovation, transforming the school from a small business-focused academy into a full-fledged, independent university that offers a diverse range of academic and cocurricular programs across eleven faculties.

When I first joined the university, the Caucasus School of Business was a collaborative entity operating under the auspices of three state-run universities in Georgia. Under my guidance, it transitioned into an autonomous institution, expanding its educational offerings from solely business programs to include a broad spectrum of disciplines at three levels of education—bachelor's, master's, and doctoral. My strategic vision was not just to expand the institution in size but also to build a comprehensive educational ecosystem that would serve the diverse needs of students in Georgia and beyond by offering a wide range of academic programs.

Since starting with just ten students in the business school, I rapidly expanded the institution's enrollment, which now exceeds 10,000 students. My leadership came at a time when Georgia's educational system was still recovering from its Soviet-era influences. Despite these challenges, under my direction Caucasus University became the first institution in Georgia to introduce international exchange programs and double-degree opportunities—a revolutionary step that placed CU at the forefront of higher education internationalization in the country. The partnership with Georgia State University played a critical role in bringing Western-style education to the country of Georgia and setting CU apart as a model for modern education in the region.

Beyond the development of academic programs, my vision also extended to the physical and infrastructural growth of the university. A pivotal moment during this leadership was the decision to move from a rented facility to a historic campus in the heart of Tbilisi, symbolizing the university's growth and ambition. The subsequent development of a state-of-the-art modern campus and the establishment of a dynamic new campus in Batumi were further milestones that provided students with world-class learning environments. These campuses not only enhanced the student experience but also significantly raised CU's profile on the global stage, positioning it as a leading institution in the region.

In addition to transforming CU's physical infrastructure, I have played a crucial role in expanding the university's international presence. Under my leadership, CU established numerous global partnerships and became a member of several prestigious international academic networks, which created unprecedented opportunities for both students and faculty. These collaborations have helped CU attract top-tier international faculty, enabled student mobility programs, and expanded CU's reputation as a hub for academic excellence and innovation.

My leadership is characterized by a commitment to academic excellence, strategic growth, and internationalization. My efforts have not only shaped CU into one of the region's most prestigious universities, but they have also made it a beacon of progress in higher education and set the stage for future generations of students and academics to thrive.

Professional Journey

My professional journey spans multiple sectors, with leadership roles in both academia and public service. As president of Caucasus University, I have been instrumental in transforming the institution into a globally recognized center of academic excellence that offers students a dynamic and internationally respected education.

My influence on global higher education is particularly notable through my tenure as president of the International Association of University Presidents (IAUP) from 2017 to 2021. During this time, I led efforts to foster international collaborations, enhance educational standards, and expand the global reach of higher education institutions. I continued my leadership role as chairman of the IAUP Board of Directors from 2021 to 2024, solidifying my reputation as a thought leader in the sector.

My leadership extended to my role as vice mayor of Tbilisi, where I was responsible for overseeing social affairs. My initiatives focused on improving the city's social welfare systems, addressing the needs of vulnerable populations, and reducing inequality. My work in social policy contributed to enhancing the quality of life for Tbilisi's residents and creating a more inclusive environment.

In public service, I have made significant contributions as a member of the Parliament of Georgia (2004–08), through which I played a key role in shaping national policies related to education, science, culture, and foreign affairs. As deputy chairman of the Ministry of Education, Science, Culture, and Sports, and the Foreign Relations Committee, my efforts were pivotal in advancing reforms aimed at improving Georgia's education system and strengthening international relations. I was also instrumental in modernizing educational frameworks and promoting global partnerships.

In addition to my administrative and academic leadership, I have dedicated part of my career to teaching, offering courses on management concepts and the history of Georgia. My passion for education and mentorship is central to my personal mission of shaping future leaders and professionals equipped to succeed in a globalized world. My book, *History of Georgia* (2007), has been translated into several languages and is available to international students and scholars worldwide. The book offers a comprehensive exploration of Georgia's rich history that spans from ancient times to the modern era and highlights its cultural heritage, political evolution, and significant historical events. It serves as a valuable resource for anyone who is seeking a deeper understanding of Georgia's role in regional and global history.

My extensive contributions to both academia and public service have earned numerous prestigious awards. I have been honored with the Presidential Order of Excellence by the President of Georgia as well as with the Ring of Honor from the University of Applied Sciences Upper Austria. I have received honorary doctorates from esteemed institutions, including Tallinn University of Technology (Estonia), the University of Guadalajara (Mexico), and J. F. Oberlin University (Japan). My highest honor came from the University of Johannesburg at the proposal of Professor Tshilidzi Marwala, current rector of the United Nations University, who was awarded an honorary doctorate from CU.

I hold key positions on the board of directors of the World University Consortium and the European Public Law Organization. I am also a member of the Council of Representatives of the European Law and Governance School and a fellow of the World Academy of Art and Science, through which I continue to contribute to global discussions on education, governance, and public policy.

A Legacy of Innovation and Inclusion

My leadership at CU has been defined by my unique role as the institution's founding figure. Unlike typical university presidents, my journey as the dean of the Caucasus School of Business played a pivotal role in the university's early development. In its infancy, CU was shaped by my vision, determination, and unwavering commitment to educational excellence, which set the foundation for what would eventually become a renowned institution. I quite literally built CU from scratch, shaping every aspect of the university's identity, values, and structure.

My visionary leadership introduced Western-style academic integrity, transparency, and global engagement to the post-Soviet educational landscape, creating a distinctive space for CU in a region transitioning from

Soviet-era education systems. By blending Eastern European traditions with Western academic standards, I made CU a trailblazer in higher education. My approach was grounded in the understanding that a truly modern, competitive university must embrace international standards while staying firmly rooted in its local context.

My leadership strategy is centered on collaboration, innovation, and inclusion. As the university grew, my management style fostered an environment where faculty, students, and administration worked hand in hand to shape CU's trajectory. Through weekly board meetings, regular corporate retreats, and frequent cultural engagement activities, I created a dynamic and cohesive community focused on shared goals. My open-door policy allowed constant communication between all levels of the institution, ensuring that feedback, ideas, and concerns were always heard and addressed. This transparency nurtured a culture of trust and mutual respect that enabled innovation to flourish.

A key aspect of my leadership has been my commitment to gender equality and diversity in higher education. From the outset, I ensured that women played a significant role in CU's leadership, faculty, and student body. My efforts to empower women in academia and business have been particularly evident through the Leadership Excellence: Driving Organizational Change and Success program—CU's women's leadership training—which has transformed the careers of women seeking to excel in traditionally male-dominated fields. Looking ahead, CU launched an executive leadership training program for women in 2025, further underscoring my dedication to creating an equitable environment for all students, regardless of gender.

Through my leadership, CU has become a model of innovation and inclusion, building a strong reputation not only in Georgia but across the globe. My legacy is one of collaboration, transparency, and empowerment—qualities that continue to define CU's identity and its trajectory in the world of higher education.

Distinct Contributions to Leadership

My tenure as the founding leader of CU has been marked by transformative contributions that have shaped the institution into one of the most respected universities in the Caucasus region. Unlike traditional university presidents, I did not step into an established institution but had the unique opportunity to shape CU's identity from the ground up. My visionary leadership laid the foundation for a university that bridges Eastern European traditions with Western academic standards, creating an educational environment built on integrity, transparency, and global engagement.

My decision to introduce Western-style academic integrity and global engagement to the post-Soviet educational landscape was a bold and pioneering move. At a time when higher education in Georgia was still recovering from its Soviet legacy, CU became a model of modernization. My leadership was instrumental in developing a university that not only embraced international academic standards but also prepared students to thrive in an interconnected global environment.

My ability to lead the university from its humble beginnings as a small business school into a full-fledged institution that offers eleven faculties, serves over 10,000 students, and has partnerships with prestigious universities across the globe speaks volumes about my vision and commitment to innovation.

Effective Leadership Strategies and Championing Diversity and Advancement

My leadership at CU is defined by my visionary approach; unwavering commitment to innovation, inclusivity, and sustainability; and exceptional risk-taking ability. My leadership strategies have not only positioned CU as a dynamic and globally recognized institution but also reinforced my dedication to fostering a forward-thinking academic environment in which collaboration, new ideas, and global engagement thrive.

A hallmark of my leadership is my bold and strategic decision-making, often in the face of uncertainty. My willingness to take calculated risks has been instrumental in CU's success, allowing the university to pioneer initiatives that were initially met with skepticism but ultimately proved transformative. My ability to anticipate future trends and act decisively, even when support was lacking, has been a key factor in CU's growth. Whether it was establishing international partnerships during Georgia's post-Soviet transition or implementing progressive educational reforms, my foresight has consistently propelled CU forward.

My approach to internationalization exemplifies this forward-thinking mindset. At a time when Georgian higher education was still rooted in Soviet-era practices, I championed the integration of global academic standards and partnerships. CU became the first Georgian university to offer international exchange opportunities and double-degree programs, positioning itself as a leader in higher education reform. These pioneering efforts allowed CU to align with Western academic norms while maintaining a strong connection to the region's cultural heritage.

My leadership also strongly focuses on empowering women and promoting gender equality. Under my guidance, CU has not only advanced gender equality within its governance and academic structures but has also taken significant steps to support womens entrepreneurship. CU's acceleration programs have become key players in promoting women-led start-ups by offering mentorship, resources, and funding opportunities that are specifically tailored to support women entrepreneurs. These programs aim to create a thriving ecosystem for women business leaders that fosters innovation and entrepreneurship among young women. CU also strives to raise awareness about the importance of gender-inclusive entrepreneurship by hosting events and workshops that highlight the challenges and successes of women in the business world. This is in line with CU's broader goal of creating a gender-equitable environment where leadership opportunities are available to all, regardless of gender.

Another defining aspect of my leadership is my emphasis on open communication and collaboration at all levels of the university. Recognizing that effective leadership requires transparency and active engagement from all stakeholders, I introduced weekly board meetings and regular corporate retreats. These sessions foster open dialogue, ensuring alignment among faculty, administrators, and students while reinforcing a shared vision for CU's future.

I also understand the power of cultural engagement in building a strong academic community. By strategically integrating cultural events and collaborative activities into university life, I have cultivated an inclusive environment that values diverse perspectives. This commitment to inclusivity is further reflected in CU's policies, which promote gender equality and leadership opportunities for women. Under my guidance, CU became a signatory of the Women's Empowerment Principles, reinforcing its commitment to fostering women's leadership. Among CU's twenty-five board members, nineteen are women; of its five vice presidents, three are women; and of its eleven deans, eight are women. One of the most notable initiatives in this area is the women's leadership training program, which empowers women to excel in leadership roles across academia and business.

My leadership is also distinguished by my commitment to sustainability. I have made it a priority to integrate sustainable practices into CU's operations and academic programs, ensuring that students are not only equipped with professional knowledge but also with a strong sense of social and environmental responsibility. My efforts to align CU's strategic framework with the United Nations Sustainable Development Goals have led to the development of programs and partnerships that promote green technologies, sustainable business models, and socially responsible initiatives.

Further, I have established international expert councils to embed interdisciplinary and global perspectives into CU's leadership. These councils, composed of thought leaders from around the world, provide valuable insights that guide CU's strategic direction, ensuring that the university remains globally competitive while addressing local challenges. By integrating diverse viewpoints, I have successfully positioned CU as a leader in higher education that is capable of adapting to the evolving demands of an interconnected world.

My leadership exemplifies the power of vision, the courage to take risks, and the spirit of resilience. My ability to make bold decisions, even in the face of uncertainty, has been instrumental in CU's rise as a premier institution in the region. By fostering innovation, inclusivity, sustainability, and global engagement, I have created a university that not only prepares students for the future but actively shapes it.

Personal Identity and Leadership

My leadership is deeply rooted in my personal identity and diverse experiences, which have shaped the way I lead and interact with others. My background as both an academic and an active participant in Georgia's public life plays a significant role in shaping my leadership style. My extensive career has imbued me with a unique blend of practical governance skills, cultural sensitivity awareness, and deep commitment to shaping educational excellence in Georgia and beyond.

My personal identity is influenced by my strong connection to Georgian heritage, keen understanding of international academic standards, and firm belief in the importance of academic integrity and global engagement. Raised in a country that transitioned from Soviet control to independence, I experienced firsthand the challenges of rebuilding and redefining national identity and institutions. This formative period has greatly influenced my view of leadership by emphasizing the need to adapt and evolve in a rapidly changing global landscape.

My leadership style reflects my multicultural experiences and multilingual abilities, which have allowed me to effectively communicate with diverse groups around the world. I am fluent in Georgian, English, French, Russian, and Turkish, and I have navigated a variety of cultural and professional settings; I am highly adaptable. This adaptability is evident in my leadership at CU, where I have successfully built a university that is inclusive, forward-thinking, and internationally oriented. My ability to integrate local values with global perspectives has been instrumental in creating a unique academic environment at CU that bridges Eastern European and Western traditions.

I am widely respected for my integrity, accessibility, and visionary leadership. Colleagues, students, and partners frequently highlight my open-door policy, my active engagement with faculty, and my commitment to social and academic responsibility. My approachability and willingness to listen to diverse viewpoints have made me not only a leader but also a mentor to many within the CU community. I am seen as a symbol of transparency and a commitment to positive change—qualities that inspire those around me to actively contribute to the university's growth and direction.

Advice for Aspiring Leaders

Based on my extensive experience in leadership roles, both in academia and government, I offer valuable advice to fellow presidents, rectors, and chancellors who are aiming to succeed in their leadership positions:

- Prioritize open communication and collaboration: One of the most important aspects of leadership is creating an environment in which communication is transparent and collaboration is encouraged.

As leaders, we must ensure that everyone feels heard and valued. Implementing regular opportunities for open dialogue, such as weekly meetings or feedback sessions, helps align the institution's efforts and build trust within the community.

- Lead by example: Leadership is not about issuing directives from above. It's about leading by example. Demonstrating the values you wish to instill in your institution—such as integrity, transparency, and inclusivity—through your actions is key to gaining the respect of your colleagues, students, and staff.
- Embrace change and innovation: Higher education is evolving at a rapid pace, and leaders must be at the forefront of innovation. Embrace change, explore new educational models, and keep pushing the boundaries of what is possible. It's crucial to stay adaptable and open-minded, especially in times of crisis or transformation.
- Empower your team: A strong leader surrounds themselves with capable individuals and empowers them to take ownership of their work. Delegating responsibility and fostering a culture of trust can drive innovation and increase productivity. Your team should be an extension of your vision, not just people carrying out your orders.
- Foster inclusivity: Leadership should be inclusive and diverse. I strongly believe in creating environments in which everyone feels respected—regardless of their background. Diversity is not just a moral imperative; it's a strength that brings creativity, fosters innovation, and offers new perspectives.

Guidance for Aspiring Leaders

For individuals who are aspiring to become presidents, rectors, or chancellors, I share the following guidance based on my personal journey and leadership experiences:

- Develop a deep understanding of your institution: Before assuming a leadership role, invest time in understanding your institution's history, culture, and unique challenges. This will give you the insights needed to lead with purpose and integrity. Leadership is not about imposing a personal agenda; it's about guiding the institution toward its goals in a way that respects its traditions while preparing it for the future.

- Cultivate emotional intelligence: The ability to understand and manage your emotions, as well as the emotions of others, is essential for effective leadership. Emotional intelligence helps you to navigate difficult conversations, resolve conflicts, and connect with individuals on a personal level. As a leader, your ability to empathize and build rapport is just as important as your ability to make strategic decisions.
- Prepare for challenges and failures: No leadership journey is without its challenges. There will be setbacks and obstacles. The key is to learn from them and remain resilient. Failure is often the best teacher, as it pushes you to rethink strategies and grow. Don't shy away from difficult situations—face them head-on and use them as opportunities for improvement.
- Build a global network: In today's interconnected world, it's important to build relationships with colleagues, alumni, and institutions across the globe. Engaging with graduates—both from your own institution and others—offers valuable insights, mentorship opportunities, and professional connections. These relationships not only foster academic partnerships but also provide a broader understanding of different educational systems and leadership models.
- Be authentic and true to your values: Leadership requires authenticity. It's important to stay true to your values, especially when faced with pressure or opposition. Your authenticity will resonate with others and inspire them to trust in your leadership. Stay grounded in your principles, and don't be afraid to take a stand for what is right.
- Never stop learning: Leadership is a continuous journey of self-improvement. Never stop learning from others, whether they are peers, mentors, or those you lead. Stay curious, seek feedback, and strive to improve your skills. The best leaders are those who are constantly evolving.
- Leverage the power of alumni: Alumni are a vital part of any institution's global community and serve as ambassadors, mentors, and collaborators. By staying connected with alumni, you gain access to a wealth of experience, industry insights, and career opportunities. Engaging with alumni can facilitate knowledge sharing, create pathways for professional growth, and strengthen institutional ties across borders.

Conclusion

My reflections on my own leadership journey highlight the importance of integrity, inclusivity, collaboration, and adaptability. My success as a leader is attributed to my ability to embrace change, foster open communication, and stay grounded in my values. I emphasize that effective leadership is not about commanding from the top but instead about empowering others and creating an environment in which everyone can contribute to the collective success of the institution.

For aspiring leaders, my advice focuses on building strong relationships, cultivating emotional intelligence, and staying authentic to one's values. By following these principles, leaders can pave the way for long-lasting success, sustainable growth, and positive impact within their institutions.

Reference

Silogava, Valeri, and Kakha Shengelia. 2007. *History of Georgia: From the Ancient Times Through the "Rose Revolution."* Caucasus University Publishing House.

13 Rooted in Legacy, Guided by Wisdom

Ichiro Tanioka

President, Osaka University of Commerce (Japan)

Introducing My Institution

Japan is a country that is known to have no single strong leader in any organization or entity, and decisions are usually made by consensus or following the majority. Naturally, reaching any decision is very time-consuming, and drastic reform is hardly able to be achieved if it is contradictory to traditional routines or values. So, please do not expect much from my words, since I'm just a president of a small, private university in Japan.

Currently, there are 811 universities in Japan. Among these 811 universities, eighty-six are national, 101 are public (state or municipally owned), and the remaining 624 universities are private (MEXT 2024). Most of those private institutions are small, with fewer than 5,000 students enrolled.

Tanioka Gakuen Educational Foundation (TGE-F) is a private, not-for-profit entity that manages several educational institutions. TGE-F was established in 1928 and currently includes two universities, three high schools, and one kindergarten in Osaka and Hyōgo prefectures in Japan. I am the chancellor of TGE-F.

Osaka University of Commerce (OUC), where I serve as the president in addition to the chancellor, has three undergraduate departments: economics, management, and public administration. OUC offers two master's degrees and one doctoral degree.

Kobe Design University (KDU) is another university located in Kobe, the capital of Hyōgo prefecture. KDU focuses on environmental design (architecture and landscape), manufacturing (products and crafts), visual design, and media arts (filmmaking, manga/animation, graphics, and other arts), established in 1989.

There are also three high schools in TGE-F; one is in proximity to OUC, while the other two are in other cities within the same Osaka prefecture. All of them are coeducation institutions that are renowned for their athletic programs. Another kindergarten is under the umbrella of TGE-F.

The mission statement of TGE-F is to foster students who can perform important roles in society, which is a kind of broad and ambiguous mission, you may think. Therefore, I have created four concrete pillars as a modern interpretation of the mission. They are kindness and courtesy, fundamental and practical learning, ability to think flexibly, and positive and enjoyable life.

Leadership Tenure

I have served as the president of OUC for the past twenty-eight years. Because TGE-F is a private entity, the board of directors appoints the presidents and principals of each school. My father was the chair of the board when I was appointed. Prior to me, the president of OUC was my father. And before my father, it was my grandfather. Yes, it's a family business.

The most defining moment of my tenure was when I created the Department of Public Administration, a new department within OUC. Many said that it would be a big failure; however, it has proven to be successful. A mark of success is that many other universities followed the trend of creating departments in public administration and copied our curriculum.

Professional Journey

As mentioned before, I'm the third generation of TGE-F leadership. I am the first son of the first son (my father) of the first son (my grandfather); naturally, in Japanese tradition and culture, I had been expected to be a chair of TGE-F unless there were reasons that I should not be.

My family was educationally oriented, and naturally, I was well educated so that I could also take some roles in the academic world (if possible) in addition to managing TGE-F.

Fortunately, I am the type of person who is fond of reading books and engaging in different academic fields. I have researched many different subjects (and I feel I could do well in some of them). Although I earned my PhD in sociology (more specifically, criminology), I have published books in the fields of mathematics, geography, puzzles, law, science fiction, history of games, world history of calendars, gambling studies, research methods, sports betting, and several criminology publications. I have either contributed to or written more than seventy books and at least forty of them are my personal publications.

Effective Leadership Strategies

As a leader, I should behave as if I am capable and confident to make important decisions. To do so, there are several customs or practices that I usually keep in mind when I make a speech in front of other people, such as professors, faculties, staff, or students.

First, the speech must be short and condensed. A true leader should know what to do, how to do them, and why. I am not sure if I am a capable decision-maker, but at least I am a confident leader who believes in what to do, how to do it, and why we should do it.

Second, to make a speech, I do not prepare a script. The contents that I shall say in the speech are always in my head. Because I do not read a script, I can look at faces in the audience or even ask questions to individuals. I occasionally take a pause, if necessary, so that the listeners can concentrate more. Moreover, I sometimes even change the contents while I'm speaking, according to the response and attitudes of listeners.

In summary, to maintain my leadership, I seek to appear as a strong and confident leader through my words and through my presentation. So far, it looks like it's working.

Personal Identity and Perception

Even for an average size university (for Japan), there are more than 100 professors and faculties in OUC. To be a leader of them, one should be respected by them. Though I am not conscious about how my leadership style is perceived, I tried to become one who is respected.

Max Weber—a German sociologist and political economist—stated that there are three sources of power for leadership: namely, tradition, charisma, and legitimacy. As I mentioned, I was born into a family who possessed traditional power because my grandfather was the founder. I felt the obligation to be a legitimate leader, understanding that charismatic power would come later if I were qualified.

I tried to teach as many classes as possible, and I studied many subjects in addition to my primary discipline. I also tried to write influential books and papers and undertake many roles both internally and externally, so that I could increase my scope of influence.

Outside, for my institution, I have been appointed to many positions. For example, the Ministry of Education, Culture, Sports, Science, and Technology (MEXT) has appointed me to three influential committee positions that envision and recommend the direction of Japan's national higher educational policies. Several public entities also appointed me as a board or committee member aligned with MEXT's mission; this means that I receive important policy information before it is released. Having early and frequent access to this information helps me lead and add value to TGE-F.

Advice for Fellow Leaders

I address the students during matriculation or commencement ceremonies for all schools of TGE-F. In these cases, I speak not only to students but also to their parents and—more importantly—to all the faculty and staff. For students, I seek to share and remind them of the mission and purpose of TGE-F.

Naturally, the faculty and staff hear the same notion of the mission and purpose several times. That is not bad at all, since an important part of my job as a leader is to show the direction we are heading. The direction should be clearly identified and offer a common message for everyone.

A very important aspect in Japanese culture is that the leader repeatedly says either the same or similar concepts without variation. To do so, one must hold a firm and concrete philosophy in one's own mind. If one has a clear philosophy of how to live, how the society should be, how the world should be harmonized, et cetera, there should already be an answer to the questions of how education should be and how one should act as a leader in the educational world.

Given this leadership philosophy, my advice is that your role as a leader is to let people go in the same direction, and for that purpose, you must have a firm and concrete philosophy within yourself. When you speak, try not to deviate from that.

Guidance for Aspiring Leaders

We ought to know leaders are lonely in nature. Of course, one leader may have a family, friends, and many followers who admire the leader. What I mean by lonely is about decision-making and taking responsibility for the result.

I believe there are three important attributes that every good leader must have. Namely, they are knowledge and wisdom, decision-making skills, and humane characteristics. Let me explain briefly.

As a leader, especially inside any academic circle, you must be knowledgeable of many issues. There is no shortcut to being a knowledgeable person; so, I must repeat that you should keep reading, keep writing, keep listening, and keep studying every day of your life. Knowledge that can be researched and achieved through books (such as the dictionary), smartphones, and internet environment (such as artificial intelligence) are fine and important, but the application of varying knowledge is more important. This application ability can be called wisdom, and it is a key aspect for a leader.

Even if a leader knows the right direction in which the organization should go, they must decide and let others move toward the right direction. This is the decision-making part of leadership. It's sad to see someone full of knowledge and new ideas who cannot decide or cannot declare and persuade others. That type of person can be a good staff officer or adviser to a leader but is not a leader by themselves.

A leader may research, check the experience, or seek advice from others. But the final decision must be made alone. In that sense, a leader is very isolated and lonely.

The last attribution, humanity, is the most important of all three. Even if a leader is knowledgeable, a good decision-maker, and capable of directing the faculty and staff, the organization will not be highly successful if they are not respected and loved by them. Leaders make countless number of decisions, and the leader may still fail. If they are respected and loved—say, if they are good at the aspect of humanity—their failure may not be so harshly judged, or those failures may be taken as just unlucky. But, if they are arrogant in nature, the result may not be such a soft landing. The organization is weak in nature under such a fragile leader.

These are my notions of the three necessary attributes for successful leadership. You do not have to follow all, but you should have your own concrete notion instead. Otherwise, one may not be a true leader.

Championing Diversity and Advancement

I do not personally think that it's a problem for some groups to be underrepresented if opportunities are given equally. OUC, of which I am in charge, does not adopt any affirmative action for admissions nor any other special treatment because we believe any artificial implementation of this distribution would not be the final resolution for society. Of course, any discrimination should not be allowed.

The result of attributable distribution, I admit, may not be equal. Further, in society today, people are classified (or diversified) across many sub- or sub-sub–groups for complex reasons. Women are just one of those subgroups.

Traditions and cultures dare not be evaluated by one standard only which originates from one value. For instance, Japanese housewives and househusbands usually deal with the financial matters of the family. Men and women who work get their allowance only.

I must admit, Japanese women are underrepresented in many important positions. The biggest reason for this is the persistent social pressure that women do not have to compete with men. Even female students' mothers say to their daughters, "You are a woman—you do not have to compete so hard with others." For example, women are underrepresented in an assembly, yet women are the majority in the voting population. This means that many women do not vote for candidates from the same gender. This view should be changed in certain ways, but I believe artificial correction is not an answer. The answer should be the contents of education but not the enrollment impacting the educational system. Anyone coming from any demographic or background can break the glass ceiling if only by one's effort and ability. I am hoping such a day will come in the near future; am I dreaming?

Reference

MEXT (Ministry of Education, Culture, Sports, Science, and Technology). 2024. "About Public Universities." Last modified May 1, 2024. https://www.mext.go.jp/a_menu/koutou/kouritsu/.

Index

Contributor Biographies

Amine Bensaid

President, Al Akhawayn University in Ifrane (Morocco)

Amine Bensaid is president of Al Akhawayn University in Ifrane (AUI). He is also a computer science professor and serves on several educational boards, both in Morocco and internationally. He has held various academic leadership positions, including president of Université Mundiapolis de Casablanca and various roles at AUI. With a PhD from the University of South Florida and research stints at Carnegie Mellon University and Delft University of Technology, his research has focused on artificial intelligence (neural networks, fuzzy pattern recognition, and data mining). His current interests lie in the role of higher education in helping Gen Z to thrive in the twenty-first century. Bensaid is a Fulbright scholar and a member of multiple honor societies.

Main fields of research: Artificial intelligence (in particular, neural networks, fuzzy pattern recognition, and data mining)

Major publications to date

Alaoui, Salim Mounir, Tarek A. El-Ghazawi, Ophir Frieder, Abdelghani Bellaachia, and Amine Bensaid. "Mapping Tasks onto Nodes: A Parallel Local Neighborhood Approach." *Future Generation Computer Systems* 17, no. 4 (2001): 397–403.

Bensaid, Amine M., Lawrence O. Hall, James C. Bezdek, et al. "Validity-Guided (Re)Clustering with Applications to Image Segmentation." *IEEE Transactions on Fuzzy Systems* 4, no. 2 (June 1996): 112–23.

Bensaid, Amine M., Lawrence O. Hall, James C. Bezdek, and Laurence P. Clarke. "Partially Supervised Clustering for Image Segmentation." *Pattern Recognition* 29, no. 5 (May 1996): 859–71.

Hall, L.O., A.M. Bensaid, L.P. Clarke, R.P. Velthuizen, M.S. Silbiger, and J.C. Bezdek. "A Comparison of Neural Network and Fuzzy Clustering Techniques in Segmenting Magnetic Resonance Images of the Brain." *IEEE Transactions on Neural Networks* 3, no. 5 (1992): 672–82.

Skarmeta, Antonio, Amine Bensaid, and Nadia Tazi. "Text Categorization with Semi-Supervised Agglomerative Hierarchical Clustering." *International Journal of Intelligence Systems* 15, no. 7 (July 2000): 633–46.

Juan Camilo Montoya Bozzi

Rector, Universidad Autónoma de Bucaramanga (Colombia)

Juan Camilo Montoya Bozzi has been rector of Universidad Autónoma de Bucaramanga (UNAB) since 2018. He holds a business administration degree from Universidad de los Andes and an MBA from American University's Kogod School of Business. He also completed executive programs at INALDE Business School and UNAB. His previous roles include chief executive officer of the Chamber of Commerce of Bucaramanga, URBANAS (real estate and construction), and Promisión (private equity) and was general manager of the National Business Association of Colombia. He is currently a board member of Instituto Colombiano de Crédito Educativo y Estudios Técnicos en el Exterior, Prosantander, Asociación Colombiana de Universades, Red Universitaria Mutis, and UNIRED. His work focuses on regional development, institutional transformation, and strategic leadership in higher education.

Main fields of research: Academic background in business administration; main interests in strategy, leadership, higher education management, regional competitiveness and development, and university-industry collaboration

Tim Brailsford

Vice Chancellor and President, Bond University (Australia)

Tim Brailsford currently serves as the seventh vice chancellor of Bond University, a role he has held since 2012. Located on the Gold Coast, Bond University is Australia's first and most highly ranked private university, known for its excellence in teaching and the student experience. His career in higher education includes roles as dean of several business schools in Australia. Professor Brailsford has held numerous visiting roles in Europe, the UK, North America, and Asia. He has been elected as president of several professional and learned societies, and he holds various professional fellowships. He is the author of several books in the field of investment.

Major fields of research: Financial economics, particularly the pricing and understanding of price movements in financial markets and the volatility of financial asset prices and estimating risk premia.

Major publications to date

Brailsford, Tim, ed. *Business Education in the Asia-Pacific: Contexts and Challenges*. Asia-Pacific Business School, 2011.

Brailsford, Tim, Richard Heaney, and Chris Bilson. *Investments: Concepts and Applications*, 5th ed. Cengage Learning Australia, 2014.

Shawn Chen

President, World Federation of United Nations Associations; President, International Association of University Presidents; and Founder and Chairman of the Board, Sias University (China)

Shawn Chen is an advocate of lifelong learning who has dedicated more than forty years to education. He holds a bachelor's degree from Chongqing University, a master's degree from Linfield University, and MBAs from Willamette University and the University of California, Los Angeles. In 2005, Chen earned a certificate for the Institute for Management and Leadership in Education at Harvard Graduate School of Education.

He holds honorary doctorates from the University of Humanistic Studies (1997) in California, the University of the Cordilleras (2011) in the Philippines, Caucasus University (2014) in Georgia, Danubius International University in Romania (2015), the University of West Los Angeles (2019), and Linfield University (2024).

Main fields of research: Internationalization of education, higher education management, and the study and translation of Chinese history and literature

Major publications to date

Wu, Colin, and Shawn Chen, eds. and trans. *Dao de Jing by Laozi, Recitation Version*. Hong Kong Intellectual Property Exchange, 2021.

Wu, Colin, and Shawn Chen, eds. and trans. *Zizhi Tongjian a.k.a. The Comprehensive Mirror to Aid in Government*. Hong Kong Intellectual Property Exchange, 2023.

Md. Sabur Khan

Founder and Chairman, Daffodil International University (Bangladesh)

Md. Sabur Khan is the founder and chairman of Daffodil International University and Daffodil Group. A visionary leader, he pioneered entrepreneurship education and digital transformation in Bangladesh's higher education sector. As president of the Association of the Universities of Asia and the Pacific and chairman of the Association of Prive Universities of Bangladesh, he champions innovation, inclusion, and cross-border academic collaboration. His initiatives—ranging from agentic artificial intelligence in education to skill-based entrepreneurship—have impacted thousands globally. He is an author, researcher, and speaker who actively promotes youth leadership and sustainable innovation across Asia and beyond. Kahn has published numerous research articles on innovation ecosystems, microcredentialing, start-up incubation, and the role of private universities in sustainable development in international journals. He is a regular contributor to national and international forums, including publications on agentic artificial intelligence in education, technical and vocational education transformation, and smart university models.

Main fields of research: Entrepreneurship education, digital transformation in higher education, agentic artificial intelligence and future skills, and university-industry collaboration models to drive socioeconomic development and poverty alleviation

Major publications to date

Kahn, Md. Sabur. *Entrepreneurship Development in Bangladesh: A Case Study Based Approach.*

Kahn, Md. Sabur, ed. *Handbook of Entrepreneurship Development.* Dhaka Chamber of Commerce and Industry, 2013.

Kahn, Md. Sabur. *A Journey Towards Entrepreneurship.* Daffodil International University Press, 2017.

Fernando León García

President, CETYS University (Mexico), and Chair, International Association of University Presidents Board of Directors

Fernando León García has been president of CETYS University since 2010, leading the institution to receive multiple US accreditations (such as from the Western Association of Schools and Colleges (WASC) Senior College and University Commission, the Accreditation Council for Business Schools and Programs, and ABET) and to become one of the most internationalized universities in Mexico. He is the chair of the International Association of University Presidents' board of directors for the term from 2024 to 2027.

In addition, he serves or has served on national and international boards or advisory groups, including WASC, The Council of Independent Colleges, the Association of International Education Administrators, CASE (the Council for Advancement and Support of Education), NAFSA: Association of International Educators, the Hispanic Association of Colleges and Universities, Federación de Instituciones Mexicanas Particulares de Educación Superior, Asociación Nacional de Universidades e Instituciones de Educación Superior, Santander Universidades México, the Association of Governing Boards of Universities and Colleges, the Consortium for North American Higher Education Collaboration, the International Association of Universities, and the American Council on Education.

Major publications to date

León García, Fernando. "Imagine una Educacion Superior Internacionalizada." In *El Futuro de las Universidades: Edición México*, edited by Victoria Galán-Muros, Arno Meerman, Balzhan Orazbayeva, et al. University Industry Innovation Network, 2021.

León García, Fernando. "Emerging Trends for Leaders in the Post Pandemic Era." *On the Horizon: The International Journal of Learning Futures* 33, no. 1 (February 2023): 6–10.

León García, Fernando, Sergio M. Alcocer, Taylor Eighmy, and Santa J. Ono. "Higher Education Collaboration in North America: A Review of the Past and a Potential Agenda for the Future." In *North America 2.0: Forging a Continental Future*, edited by Tom Long and Alan Bersin. North American Institutes at the Woodrow Wilson International Center for Scholars, 2022.

León García, Fernando, and Arturo Cherbowski Lask. *Leadership Responses to COVID-19: A Global Survey of College and University Leadership*. International Association of University Presidents and Santander Universidades, 2021.

Merola, Rachael, Fernando León García, and Arturo Cherbowski Lask. *Global Perspectives of College & University Leaders in the Post Pandemic Era*. International Association of University Presidents and Santander Universidades, 2024.

Devorah Lieberman

President Emerita, University of La Verne (United States)

Devorah Lieberman is a visionary and accomplished leader who is recognized for her contributions to higher education, health care, and business in the United States and globally. She served as the eighteenth president of the University of La Verne from 2011 to 2023, making history as the first woman to hold this position in the institution's 135-year history. Currently, she holds the title of president emerita at the University of La Verne and principal of Lieberman & Associates, LLC. Since her retirement from the presidency, Lieberman continues to make an indelible impact through consulting, leadership, and strategic advisory roles, as well as her dedication to advancing education, health, business, and community initiatives.

Main fields of research: Intercultural communication, higher education, and leadership

Major publications to date

Lieberman, Devorah. "The Role of the President: Leading by Wearing Bifocals Through the Pandemic and Beyond." In *The Vitality and Power of Higher Education*, edited by Scott D. Miller and Marylouise Fennell. President to President. Virginia Wesleyan University, 2021.

Lieberman, Devorah. "The College President's Role During Times of Crisis." *Higher Education Today*, November 28, 2023. https://www.higheredtoday.org/2023/11/28/the-college-presidents-role-during-times-of-crisis/.

Lieberman, Devorah. "Wearing Leadership Bi-Focals in the Post-Pandemic University." *On the Horizon: The International Journal of Learning Futures* 31, no. 1 (February 2023): 24–29.

Lieberman, Devorah. "Beyond Crisis Management: How Presidents Can Create a Campus Where Everyone Belongs." *Higher Education Today*, February 11, 2024.

https://www.higheredtoday.org/2024/02/11/beyond-crisis-management-how-presidents-can-create-a-campus-where-everyone-belongs/.

Lieberman, Devorah. "Beyond March: Supporting Women on the Path to the College Presidency." *Higher Education Today*, April 3, 2024. https://www.higheredtoday.org/2024/04/03/beyond-march/.

Lieberman, Devorah. "Cultivating a Culture of Civility and Meaningful Dialogue on Campus during Elections." *Higher Education Today*, March 19, 2024. https://www.higheredtoday.org/2024/03/19/cultivating-a-culture-of-civility/.

Lieberman, Devorah. "Making Authentic Optimism the New Normal." *Higher Education Today*, October 1, 2024. https://www.higheredtoday.org/2024/10/01/making-authentic-optimism-the-new-normal/.

Lieberman, Devorah. "The Power of Personal Story Telling in Higher Education Leadership." *Higher Education Today*, December 2, 2024. https://www.higheredtoday.org/2024/12/02/the-power-of-personal-storytelling/.

Lieberman, Devorah. "Strategic Presidential Leadership: Addressing the Value of Institutional Mergers and Alignments." LinkedIn, September 3, 2024.

Lieberman, Devorah. "Strategic Presidential Leadership and Wrap-Around Student Services." *Higher Education Today*, April 19, 2024. https://www.higheredtoday.org/2024/04/19/wrap-around-student-services/.

Lieberman, Devorah. "Thriving Communities Now: A Presidential Imperative for Higher Education." The Phoenix Philanthropy Group, September 5, 2025. https://phoenixphilanthropy.com/resource/thriving-communities-a-presidential-imperative/.

Lieberman, Devorah, and Shannon Capaldi. "Brain Remain: Shifting the Paradigm of Pride." *The Future of Urban and Metropolitan Universities* 30, no. 4 (2019): 26–34.

Lieberman, Devorah A., and Cassia Freedland. "Successful Models and Practices – Wagner College (New York)." In *Transforming Undergraduate Education: Theory That Compels and Practices That Succeed*, edited by Donald W. Harward. Rowman & Littlefield Publishers, 2011.

Lieberman, Devorah, Fernando León García, and International Association of University Presidents. *Spotlighting Female Leadership: Strategies, Stories, Perspectives*. International Association of University Presidents, 2024.

Lieberman, Devorah, AJ Prager, and Richard Tollefson. *The Sum Is Greater Than Its Parts: Synergies in Advancement Through Higher Education Mergers*. The Phoenix Philanthropy Group, 2025.

Ricardo Mairal Usón

Rector Magnificó, Universidad Nacional de Educación a Distancia (Spain)

Ricardo Mairal Usón has been a professor of linguistics in the Department of Foreign Languages since 2002 and rector magnificó at UNED since 2018. His research interests lie in the fields of linguistic theory, knowledge representation, computational linguistics, and neurolinguistics, with a particular focus on clinical aspects and cognitive deficits associated with neurodegenerative diseases. He has participated as a speaker at numerous conferences on theoretical and applied linguistics and has published more than ninety papers in national and international forums.

He was president of the Spanish Society for Applied Linguistics from 2011 to 2017. At UNED, he served as vice-rector for research from 2013 to 2016 and vice-rector for faculty and planning from 2016 to 2018.

Main fields of research: Theoretical linguistics, natural language processing, and neurolinguistics

Major publications to date

Bentley, Delia, Ricardo Mairal Usón, Wataru Nakamura, and Robert D. Van Valin Jr. eds. *The Cambridge Handbook of Role and Reference Grammar*. Cambridge University Press, 2023.

Bosque, Ignacio, and Ricardo Mairal. "Definiciones Mínimas." In *Estudios de lingüística española: Homenaje a Manuel Seco*, edited by Félix Rodríguez González. Universidad de Alicante, 2012.

Bosque, Ignacio, and Ricardo Mairal. "Hacia una organización conceptual del definiens: Capas nocionales del adverbio *arriba*." In *Lexicografía Hispánica del Siglo XXI: Nuevos Proyectos y Perspectivas: Homenaje al Profesor Cristobal Corrales Zumbado*, edited by Dolores Corbella, Josefa Dorta, Alejandro Fajardo Aguirre, Laura Izquierdo, Javier Medina López, and Antonia Nelsi Torre. Arco Libros, 2013.

Cortés Rodríguez, Francisco José, and Ricardo Mairal. "Building an RRG Computational Grammar." *Onomazein* 34 (December 2016): 86–117. DOI: 10.7764/onomazein.34.22.

Mairal Usón, Ricardo. "Formal and Functional Approaches to Grammar." In *The Encyclopedia of Applied Linguistics*, vol. 4, edited by Carol A. Chapelle. Wiley-Blackwell, 2012.

Mairal Usón, Ricardo. "A Computational Implementation of Idiomatic and Non-Idiomatic Constructions." *Revista Signos: Estudios de Lingüística* 50, no. 94 (2017): 241–64. DOI: 10.4067/S0718-09342017000200241.

Mairal-Usón, Ricardo. "La lingüística clínica." *Revista Española de Lingüística* 51, no. 2 (July–December 2021): 159–80. https://doi.org/10.31810/rsel.51.2.10.

Mairal-Usón, Ricardo, and Francisco Cortés-Rodríguez. "Automatically Representing TExt Meaning via an Interlingua-Based System (ARTEMIS). A Further Step towards the Computational Representation of RRG." *Journal of Computer-Assisted Linguistic Research* 1, no. 1 (2017): 61–87.

Mairal Usón, Ricardo, and Pamela Faber. "Linguistic Research in the 21st Century: Looking Beyond." In *Applied Linguistics and Knowledge Transfer: Employability, Internationalisation, and Social Challenges*, edited by Ana Bocanegra-Valle. Peter Lang, 2020.

Mairal, Ricardo, and Carlos Periñán Pascual. "Representing Constructional Schemata in FunGramKB Grammaticon." In *Explorations of the Syntax-Semantics Interface*, edited by Jens Fleischhauer, Anja Latrouite, and Rainer Osswald. Studies in Language and Cognition Series, vol. 3. Düsseldorf University Press, 2016.

Mairal Usón, Ricardo, and Carlos Periñán-Pascual. "Multilingualism and Conceptual Modelling." *Círculo de Lingüística Aplicada a la Comunicación* 66 (2016): 244–77. http://dx.doi.org/10.5209/CLAC.52774.

Periñán Pascual, Carlos, and Ricardo Mairal Usón. "A Framework of Analysis for the Evaluation of Automatic Term Extractors." *Vigo International Journal of Applied Linguistics*, no. 15 (2018): 105–25.

Van Valin, Robert D., Jr., and Ricardo Mairal Usón. "Interfacing the Lexicon and an Ontology in a Linking Algorithm." In *Theory and Practice in Functional-Cognitive Space*, edited by María de los Ángeles Gómez González, Francisco

José Ruiz de Mendoza Ibáñez, and Francisco Gonzálvez-García. John Benjamins Publishing Company, 2014.

Gonzalo Mendieta

Rector, Universidad de Las Américas (Ecuador)

Gonzalo Mendieta has been rector of Universidad de Las Américas (UDLA) in Ecuador since 2019, following six years as academic vice rector. He holds a PhD in statistics from the University of Iowa and served as assistant professor at Wichita State University. Under his leadership, UDLA became the first Ecuadorian university to receive WASC accreditation and ranks among the country's top three institutions in scientific production. He serves as president of Ecuador's National Association of Private Universities and as a board member of the International Association of University Presidents. His statistical background uniquely informs his data-driven approach to institutional leadership and educational innovation.

Main field of research: Statistical methodologies and their applications, with a focus on econometrics, anthropometric studies, and data-driven decision-making in higher education administration

Major publications to date

Arichabala, Jacinto J., Ximena M. Córdova, and Gonzalo R. Mendieta. "Using a Multivariate Accommodation Model to Study Anthropometric Differences between Ethnic Groups in Ecuador." *Avances en Ciencias e Ingenierías* 7, no. 2 (2015): 5–11.

Boneh, Shahar, and Gonzalo R. Mendieta. "Variable Selection in Regression Models Using Principal Components." *Communications in Statistics* 23, no. 1 (1994): 197–213.

Larreategui Nardi, Carlos, Giuseppe Marzano, and Gonzalo R. Mendieta. "Preconditions for Collaboration at the Gold Coast." Paper presented at the 76th TOSOK Gangneung International Tourism Conference, South Korea, 2014.

Mendieta, Gonzalo R., Shahar Boneh, and Roxy Walsh. "A Simulation Study to Evaluate the Performance of a New Variable Selection Method in Regression." Computationally Intensive Statistical Methods: Proceedings of the 26th Symposium on the Interface. *Computing Science and Statistics* 26 (1994): 515–18.

Ortiz-Prado, Esteban, Gonzalo Mendieta, Katherine Simbaña-Rivera, et al. "Genotyped Indigenous Kiwcha Adults at High Altitude Are Lighter and Shorter Than Their Low Altitude Counterparts." *Journal of Physiological Anthropology* 41, no. 8 (2022).

Tomás D. Morales

President, California State University, San Bernardino (United States)

Tomás D. Morales has served as president of California State University, San Bernardino since 2012. A staunch advocate of empowering student success, he has championed the importance of access to higher education over his fifty-year career. Under Morales, CSUSB has earned top rankings in social mobility. In 2023, the American Association of State Colleges and Universities recognized CSUSB with its Diversity, Equity, and Inclusion Leadership Award. Morales's leadership career has been within the three largest US public university systems: The City University of New York, the California State University, and the State University of New York.

Main field of research: Educational leadership and policy

Major publications to date

Morales, Tomás D. "Comparison of Undergraduates in Good Academic Standing Who Persist and Who Depart the City College of New York." (PhD diss., The State University of New York at Albany, 1998).

Morales, Tomás D. "Circle Three: Top-Down Commitment." In *The Divine Comity: Student and Academic Affairs Collaboration*, edited by James H. Cook and Christopher A. Lewis. National Association of Student Personnel Administrators, 2007.

Vice-Chancellor and Principal, University of Johannesburg (South Africa)

Letlhokwa George Mpedi is a professor of law and the vice-chancellor and principal of the University of Johannesburg (UJ). He is a member of the Academy of Science of South Africa and holds an LLD conferred by UJ in 2006. He twice received the Deutscher Akademischer Austauschdienst award, in 2000 and 2001, for research in Germany. Before his current position, Mpedi served as deputy vice-chancellor: academic and executive dean of the law faculty at UJ. On July 29, 2023, Mpedi received an honorary doctorate from Caucasus University in Georgia.

Main fields of research: Labor and social security law, artificial intelligence and law

Major publications to date

Mpedi, Letlhokwa George. *From the Baobab to the Mosquito: Rethinking Leadership Through African Sayings*. Tracey McDonald Publishers, 2023.

Thandwa Mthembu

Vice-Chancellor and Principal, Durban University of Technology (South Africa)

Thandwa Mthembu became vice-chancellor and principal of Durban University of Technology (DUT) on October 1, 2016. He holds a PhD in mathematics from the University of the Witwatersrand, Johannesburg. He has published internationally, including co-authoring a monograph in approximation theory, and his interests expanded to higher education management. Mthembu has held various national leadership roles, such as chairing the Technological Higher Education Network South Africa. His extensive leadership and academic contributions have significantly shaped higher education in South Africa over the past thirty-seven years since he joined academia.

Main fields of research: Mathematics, education leadership and management

Major publications to date

Levin, A.L., D.S. Lubinsky, and T.Z. Mthembu. "Christoffel Functions and Orthogonal Polynomials for Erdös Weights on (−∞,∞)." *Rendiconti di Matematica, Serie VII* 14 (1994): 199–289.

Mthembu, Thandwa. *University Governance and the Knowledge Economy: Reconditioning the Engine of Development*. Development Planning Division Working Paper Series No. 3. Development Bank of Southern Africa, 2009.

Mthembu, Thandwa Z. "Quad-Helix Engagement for City and Regional Development: The Role of Universities in Governance, Leadership, and Management." In *Strategies for University Management, Volume II*, edited by J. Mark Munoz and Neal King. Business Expert Press, 2016.

Edward Peck

Former Vice-Chancellor, Nottingham Trent University, and Chair of the Board, Office for Students (United Kingdom)

Edward Peck worked at King's College London and the University of Birmingham before becoming vice-chancellor of Nottingham Trent University from 2014 to 2025. During this time, he was a member of the independent panel that produced *Review of Post-18 Education and Funding* (also known as the Augar report), was selected as the Department for Education's Higher Education Student Support Champion, and was chair of the Universities and Colleges Admissions Service. He began his career as a National Health Service manager.

Main fields of research: Organizational design, development and leadership in health and social care

Major publications to date

Peck, Edward, and Helen Dickinson. 2009. *Performing Leadership*. Palgrave Macmillan, 2009.

Peck, Edward, and Perri 6. *Beyond Delivery: Policy Implementation as Sense-Making and Settlement*. Palgrave Macmillan, 2006.

Perri 6, Nick Goodwin, Edward Peck, and Tim Freeman. *Managing Networks of Twenty-First Century Organizations*. Palgrave Macmillan, 2006.

Kakha Shengelia

President, Caucasus University (Georgia)

Kakha Shengelia, president of Caucasus University and former president and board chairman of the International Association of University Presidents, holds a PhD in history from Tallinn University of Technology in Estonia, a PhD in economics from Georgian Technical University in Georgia, and an MBA from the University of Hartford in the United States. As a former member of parliament of Georgia and vice mayor of Tbilisi, he led national and international education. Honors include the Presidential Order of Excellence; honorary doctorates from universities in Estonia, Mexico, Japan, South Africa, and India; and the Ring of Honor from the University of Applied Sciences Upper Austria. Shengelia serves on the boards of the World University Consortium, the European Public Law Organization, the European Law and

Governance School, and the Black Sea Universities Network. He is married with three children.

Main fields of research: Twentieth-century Georgian history and art

Major publications to date

Silogava, Valery, and Kakha Shengelia. *History of Georgia: From the Ancient Times Through the "Rose Revolution."* Caucasus University Publishing House, 2007.

Ichiro Tanioka

President, Osaka University of Commerce, and Chancellor, Tanioka Gakuen Educational Foundation (Japan)

Ichiro Tanioka received his BA in law from Keio University in 1980 and achieved his MPA and PhD in sociology from the University of Southern California in 1983 and 1989, respectively.

He is a permanent member of the International Association of University Presidents and served as its treasurer from 2014 to 2017. He is the vice-chairman of the University Mobility in Asia and the Pacific Japan National Committee. He has long been a member of the International Exchange Committee of the Association of Private Universities of Japan and currently serves as its chairman.

He started the Japanese General Social Surveys Project in cooperation with the Institute of Social Science at the University of Tokyo in 1999, and he aims to promote a variety of academic research by making the data available to those who are interested. He organized the Japan Academy of Integrated Resorts and Gaming Studies (previously, the Japan Academy for Gambling and Gaming Studies until September 2013). He has been an adviser for the legalization of the casino industry in Japan and gave a number of lectures regarding integrated resorts, casinos, gambling addiction, and so on.

Main fields of research: Criminology, study of gambling and integrated resorts

Major publications to date

Tanioka, Ichiro. "The Law of Luck." Published in Japanese. PHP Shinsho, 1997.

Tanioka, Ichiro. How to Prevent from Crime: What Is "Environmental Criminology"? Published in Japanese. Shinchosha Publishing, 2004.

Tanioka, Ichiro. "Data Tell a Lie: Research Method for Social Science Field." Published in Japanese. Chikumashobo, 2007.

Tanioka, Ichiro. *The Secret of Scientific Research and Data: There Are Many Deceptions in Japanese Academic Society.* Published in Japanese. PHP Institute, 2015.

Tanioka, Ichiro. "Devil's Proof: Is It Possible to Show That Something Does Not Exist?" Published in Japanese. Chikumashobo, 2021.

www.ingramcontent.com/pod-product-compliance
Ingram Content Group UK Ltd.
Pitfield, Milton Keynes, MK11 3LW, UK
UKHW022003240826
474727UK00001B/5

9 798216 383031